Listening with the Heart

Blessed

are the peacemakers;
they shall be remembered
as rays of the one
unity

The Beatitudes · Aramaic Translation

Listening with the Heart

A GUIDE FOR COMPASSIONATE LISTENING

THIRD EDITION

CAROL HWOSCHINSKY

COMPASSIONATE LISTENING PROJECT

Listening With The Heart:
A Guide for Compassionate Listening
Copyright © 2001

First edition, April 2001
Second edition, November 2001
Third edition, June 2002

Published by:
The Compassionate Listening Project
PO Box 17
Indianola, Washington, 98342 USA
(360) 297 2280
www.mideastdiplomacy.org

You may order copies of *Listening With the Heart* from:

The Compassionate Listening Project
PO Box 17, Indianola, Washington, 98342
Phone: 360-297-2280 www.compassionatelistening.org
email: office@compassionatelistening.org

ISBN # 0-9715871-0-8

The symbol of a holarchy
is used throughout this guidebook to imply
compassion is the basic principle of being upon which all increasingly
complex relationships and communication is based.

Cover design by Peter Hwoschinsky.
Cover photo by Paul Hwoschinsky.
Book design by Patricia Broersma.

It is said, the Masai
traditional greeting is

KASSERIAN INGERA
HOW ARE THE CHILDREN

this Guide Book in
Compassionate Listening
is dedicated to

THE CHILDREN

TABLE OF CONTENTS

APPENDIX

ACKNOWLEDGEMENTS

I was stunned into an awareness of the ravages of war first when I bicycled across Germany and France in the summer of 1954, nine years after the close of World War II. There was still devastation visible. Twenty five years later I visited Babi Yar in Ukraine and Camp 9 in Lithuania, both Nazi extermination sites. I listened to stories of neighbor turning against neighbor, and times when neighbors protected each other.

Later, working in Armenia, I went to Nagorno Karabach, the focus of the Armenian/Azerbaijan war. Though the enemy had fled, hatred was palpable. Shells were lying all over the fields. Fighting had been recent — and though there was a cease fire, still, there was no signed peace agreement.

And recently, my time in Israel, Gaza and the West Bank has been more of an awakening to the ravages of war in present time.

The agony actually begins when the adrenaline rush of sirens, bombs, and bullets have subsided. War is never over. The fear and the suffering continue as people account for their losses. Anger and hatred fester.

And then the heroes and heroines emerge — some recognized, many not.

This writing has been inspired by the many people, some we have met and also read about, who stood up and said, "I will not accept hatred and war".

Since the recent warfare between Israelis and Palestinians, accounts of many of these inspiring people show up daily on the internet. And countless numbers of people continue to act in obscurity.

There is the Israeli whose son was killed by Palestinians who organized a group of both bereaved Israeli and Palestinian parents whose children have been killed in this conflict. It is called Families Forum in Support of Peace and Tolerance.

There is the young Israeli soldier whose letter to his commanding officer explains his reasons for resigning from the military and his willingness to accept the consequences.

There is an Israeli peace activist who, with a small group of Israelis, moved into a Palestinian village to act as a buffer to protect the villagers and their olive trees from Israeli destruction.

There is the Committee Against House Demolitions whose members organize and occupy Palestinian homes to try to prevent their demolition and when they are destroyed, organize their rebuilding.

There is Hisham Sharabati, his Grandfather, Mother, sisters, brother, cousins, who continue to live with dignity and good-will in the midst of occupation.

There are the families who have been our hosts who try to give their young children hope for a future.

And the Women in Black, both Israeli and Palestinian, who continue the protest.

And Dr. Iyad Sarraj, Director of Palestinian Independent Commission on Human Rights, for his efforts to promulgate non-violence.

The names of all the people are too numerous to mention. They are the subject of another book. And they represent only the Israeli-Palestinian conflict.

War is drama and sets the stage for heroism. And there are less dramatic, yet difficult obstacles and conflicts of every day life, where we are asked to risk the safety of old patterns and speak our truth. Indeed, the healing of inner conflicts, healing of rancor and pain, which plays itself out in all human relationships, calls for the hero within us all to step forth even when threatened by judgement and hatred. When people are suffering, the panacea is listening.

I wish to acknowledge all of us when we remember to practice compassion.

More specifically, I wish to acknowledge:

Leah Green, friend and co-conspirator, director of The Compassionate Listening Project (formerly MidEast Citizen Diplomacy), who, through her enormous heart and strength, has guided numerous people through the hills and valleys, the ways and bi-ways of Israel, West Bank and Gaza for many years. She wisely knew Compassionate Listening was what was called for in her citizen delegations.

Gene Knudsen Hoffman whose courage and compassion continue to inspire.

Larissa Keet, soul sister and longtime associate with whom I developed this training through many years of first learning to listen to each other.

Janet Boggia, Ann Niehaus, and Larissa – our Conflict Evolution Associates – who tested many of these ideas and found they work.

My many teachers, especially Joanna Macy, Arnie Mindell, Louise Diamond, and the training staff of the Psychosynthesis Institute of San Francisco, where I first learned to listen to myself.

My husband Paul, our children, Suzanne and Peter, their partners and children, who continue to offer many opportunities for deep listening.

Appreciation for Phil Gagnon who contributed his hand calligraphy, Rona Rubin, Ginger Rilling, Carolyn and Huley Askaar, Keri Green, Darelle Novak and Marie Pace who read the manuscript and gave invaluable comments.

Libby and Len Traubman for their wisdom and support.

Peter Hwoschinsky for the cover design and much more.

And gratitude to Trish Broersma for her design of this book.

My thanks to all.

PREFACE

by Gene Knudsen Hoffman

Compassionate Listening was developed by Gene Knudsen Hoffman, International Peacemaker. She developed this tool after realizing that all parties in a conflict were wounded and needed to be heard. Her over-arching principle is that hearing each other's story reveals unhealed wounds and allows for mutual compassion and understanding. In this way, Compassionate Listening helps to build bridges between individuals and communities in conflict and can ultimately lead to reconciliation.

Reconciliation is the most difficult of peace processes because it requires the resumption of relationship between those in conflict. It means the coming together in harmony of those who have been sundered.

My sense is that if we would reconcile, we must make radically new responses to the radically new situation in a world where violence is mindless, hopeless, meaningless and almost every nation has nuclear weapons — if they don't now, they soon will. We must move beyond initiatives we formerly used, into realms we have not yet considered, not yet discovered, trusting that there are always open to us new divine possibilities.

We peace people have always listened to the oppressed and disenfranchised. That's very important. One of the new steps I think we should take is to listen to those we consider "the enemy" with the same openness, nonjudgement, and compassion we bring to those with whom our sympathies lie. Everyone has a partial truth, and we must listen to, discern, and acknowledge this partial truth in everyone — particularly those with whom we disagree.

To reconcile, we must realize that both sides to any violence are wounded, and their wounds are unhealed. From my study of post-traumatic stress disorder in Holocaust victims and Vietnam Veterans, I am persuaded that a great source of violence is our unhealed wounds.

In 1980, I had a life-changing experience. I was on a world tour of peace centers to learn what I could

bring back to the USA. Outside the London Quaker Meeting I saw a huge sign which said: "Meeting for Worship for the torturers and the tortured." I'd long known I should listen to the tortured — but listen to the torturers? I'd never thought of that.

I began wrestling with the idea that I should listen to both sides of any conflict and when I arrived in Israel I began listening to Israelis and Palestinians. I found it changed my perspectives on each. I began to practice it everywhere I went.

In 1989 my work-focus became the Middle East, and in that year a small group of us from the Fellowship of Reconciliation went to Libya to listen to the Libyans after we'd bombed Libya twice, first to kill Khadaffi and second after we'd downed two Libyan planes over Libya. We knew our government's side and we wanted to hear the other. We did.

After ten days in Tripoli, as guests of the Libyan government, we learned a lot. We met with Libyan leaders, professors, government members, religious representatives. We had new messages to present to our government from the Libyans such as "Please remove the mines you've deposited in the Sahara Desert (during World War II) — We can't do it alone; please resume conversations with our government over our differences; and please let Libyan students come to American universities."

Our government wouldn't listen to us, since we'd gone there illegally. So we wrote our articles, spoke publicly where we could, and were considered "dangerous."

My next efforts were on my own. Between 1989 and 1996, I went to Israel and Palestine seven times to listen to both sides. I listened to Israeli psychiatrists, settlers, government members, peace people, writers, publishers and plain people. In the West Bank, since I stayed in Palestinian homes, I had more opportunity to listen to the people: refugees, families, parents whose sons had been killed, some of their sons who hadn't, academics, peace leaders, and twice I met with Yassir

Arafat. Out of those experiences came Pax Christi's Just World book of 1991 called Pieces of the Mideast Puzzle.

The breakthrough for beginning to practice Compassionate Listening in the Middle East on a broader scale came in 1996 when Leah Green, then director of Earthstewards' Mid-East Citizen Diplomacy project, contacted me. She said she had read everything I'd written on Compassionate Listening and she would like to have her delegations to Israel and Palestine begin to practice it. We took a group of 18 people to Israel and Palestine in November, 1996 for a trial run. The Compassionate Listening Project has now become an independent non-profit organization, directed by Leah Green.

Compassionate Listening is adaptable to any conflict. The listening requires a particular attitude. it is non-judgmental, non-adversarial, and seeks the truth of the person questioned, it also seeks to see through any masks of hostility and fear to the sacredness of the individual and to discern the wounds suffered by all parties. Listeners do not defend themselves, but accept what others say as their perceptions. By listening, they validate the others' right to those perceptions.

I'm not talking about listening with the "human ear." I am talking about discerning. To discern means to perceive some thing hidden or obscure. We must listen with our "spiritual ear." This is very different from deciding in advance who is right and who is wrong, and then seeking to rectify it. And, it's very hard to listen to people whom I feel are misleading, if not lying. It is hard to listen to such different memories of the same event — hard!

Here are two definitions of reconciliation we use. Thich Nhat Hanh, the Vietnamese "monk, teacher, peace-maker, and poet, describes it as "understanding both sides." Adam Curle, senior Quaker mediator from England, says, "We must work for harmony wherever we are, to bring together what is sundered by fear, hatred, resentment, injustice, or any other conditions which divide us. ....I begin with a concept of human nature based on the

belief in a divine element within each of us, which is ever available, awaiting our call to help us restore harmony. We must remember this good exists in those we oppose."

I have since learned there are similar traditions and teachings in Judaism and Islam. In his book, Jewish Renewal, Michael Lerner reminds us that "The Book of Jonah, read in synagogues on Yom Kippur, reminds us that compassion must be extended to the enemies of the Jewish people... [which means] keeping in mind at all times that they, too, are created in the image of God, and that distortions of them that lead them to wish us ill are the product of a world of pain and cruelty that shaped them in this particular way."

From Islam comes this teaching by Abderrazak Guessoum, vice rector of the great Mosque of Paris. "...Islam is tolerance, service, and mercy...though it may surprise many non-Muslims to learn it. The Koran rejects all violence. Even the notion of Jihad - so often translated as 'holy war' - actually refers to the struggle of every Muslim not to stray from the path of obedience to the will of God revealed in the Koran."

I believe that the call is for us to see that within all people is the mystery, the Spirit/God. It is within the Afrikaaner, the Contra, the Americans, Palestinians, and Israelis — everyone. By Compassionate Listening we may awaken it and thus learn the partial truth the other is carrying.

Here is a partial process. Thich Nhat Hanh asks this of us: "In South Africa the black people suffer enormously, but the white people also suffer. If we take one side, we cannot fulfill our task of reconciliation. Can you be in touch with both sides, understanding the suffering and fears of each, telling each side about the other? Can you understand deeply the suffering of both sides?"

Finally, I treasure this quotation from the poet Longfellow: "If we could read the secret history of our enemies, we should find in each person's life sorrow and suffering enough to disarm all animosity."

INTRODUCTION

by Carol Hwoschinsky

In these times of both hope and despair, global issues impact all of humanity, and will do so for generations to come. We live in times of tremendous opportunity and tremendous difficulty. The choice is ours. Can we draw upon our human capacities to solve these problems? Can we live in peace? Are we going to protect the environment in order to survive? Can we eradicate hunger and deprivation? Can we respect our diversity and join together to solve these global challenges?

Because we are part of the problem we are also part of the solution. These challenges require a new interaction. Since each human being has a piece of the answer to our problems, we must listen to each other in new ways for solutions to make themselves known. We are required to practice new ways of interaction for our very survival.

I was a young adult of the sixties and seventies, and though there were dark clouds forming, I had a sense of hope that we could call upon our personal resources and make a difference in the world. I was part of a citizen diplomacy group, one of hundreds, who travelled to the former Soviet Union in the mid 1980's during the height of the cold war. We received formal interviews with officials at high levels of government, schools and universities. However, the real impact was with ordinary citizens we met in the streets, in restaurants, and on public transport. People were eager to talk with us, to tell us their stories, to hear ours, and to meet people from afar who were really interested in who they were. Even before "Perestroika" made it relatively safe for Soviets to converse with Americans, they were often willing to risk exposure by inviting us to share tea or vodka in their homes. Some lasting friendships ensued. It was hard to experience these hospitable people as our "enemy."

How did this happen? It happened because we opened our hearts to each other. We told our stories and we listened respectfully. I strongly believe, though it can never be proven, citizen diplomacy contributed significantly to the fall of the Iron Curtain. Quite simply, these activities helped to break stereotypes on all sides. Citizen interchange is a very powerful tool for peace and is based on the premise that peace comes through the hard work of meeting one's enemy — the human being behind the stereotype — and acknowledging one another's suffering.

However, the shadow side of these movements became obvious to me and three friends. As therapists, we recognized that often people were seeking peaceful resolution with unacknowledged anger and even violence. Striving for peaceful solutions, ignorant of the conditions of conflict, they repeated the very actions that led to the conflict in the first place. My friends and I were catalyzed to explore our approach to conflict. Through four years of exploration and study, we created a ground of trust and respect among ourselves. We followed the depths of the collaborative process and witnessed changes in our own lives. We learned how to listen. This focus became a major force in my life and work, and as a result, I have been teaching and facilitating the agreement process through conflict management, diversity training and counseling for twenty years.

During this period, I was fascinated with the public emergence of Quantum physics. Hundreds of popular books appeared. I began to teach the philosophy of wholistic health to university graduate students based on the "new physics." I was ecstatic and hopeful for the future. The whole idea of field theory and how the build-up of critical mass can tip the scales, led me to this realization: when each of us takes responsibility to live our lives with integrity, aligning with and supporting others who are doing the same, ultimately, if enough people join in, the whole picture will shift. I continue to believe this is a basic principle of life. This belief has fed my faith in life and challenges me to continue to push the limits of my humanity.

My interests and skills took me to Russia numerous times to teach Psychosynthesis, a trans-personal psychology. Later, I became involved in a non-governmental organization which had initiated a project facilitating dialogue and joint ventures between Armenia and Azerbaijan. These two former Soviet Union states had fought a bloody war and had reached a stalemate. Through this project, I spent six weeks in Armenia teaching conflict resolution skills.

Upon my return from Armenia, I met Leah Green, then Director of MidEast Citizen Diplomacy, now The Compassionate Listening Project. Compassionate Listening had just become its focus. Something clicked in me, as I had come to the realization in all my counseling and conflict resolution work that listening is at the core. I wanted to expand my listening skills in the international and ethnic arena. I have since trained the delegations going to Israel, The West Bank and Gaza, developed the curriculum and served as lead trainer.

I mention my background with the hope of showing that it is possible for ordinary, unofficial people to take this work wherever they want. The field is open and ready for citizens such as you and me to give of our talents at home and abroad.

Listening is the foundation of all relationships. Though it is something humans have done since we had ears, it continues to be a major challenge to listen when we are emotionally involved in an issue. When being heard is something we long for, why is listening so hard for us to do?

As a species, we are designed to survive at all costs. Our fight/flight response is a deeply embedded survival instinct. When we perceive someone as not being "one of us," that is, not having similar opinions which make us feel safe, we instinctively perceive that person as suspect and a potential "enemy." The stimuli comes through our senses to the root brain which perceives danger. The lymbic, emotional brain decodes this information as fear. The automatic response would be to fight or flee. However,

when we can delay the call to action and engage the neo-cortex to assess the situation, we can keep our self-protective impulses at bay. We are capable of making other choices.

Because of the evolutionary development of the human brain and nervous system, we are no longer bound by this conditioned response. We now have the freedom to hold a greater vision: that of participant and that of observer. What this means is that not only can we think, we can be aware we are thinking. We are able to delay action when we are threatened or alarmed. We have the ability to observe ourselves more objectively and we can monitor our actions in the present moment.

Recent research on the function of the heart, reported by the Heartmath project, is showing there are even more possibilities for freeing ourselves from our automatic, protective reactions. What we are now learning is that the heart has a direct effect upon the brain and our perception. The heart is more than a pump.

The heart consists of more than just muscle cells. Sixty to sixty-five percent of the heart's cells are actually neural cells, identical to those of the brain. The heart is a major center of intelligence in human beings. These cells are not only linked to every organ within our bodies, but also the heart emits an electro-magnetic field which encompasses the body and extends 8-12 feet. What we feel in our heart influences our own perceptions and physiology and has a profound affect upon all living things in our environment, as well.

This is ancient wisdom. The implications for our lives are profound. Humans can directly experience feelings of appreciation, love, compassion in our hearts and intentionally direct those electromagnetic impulses to the brain, thus counteracting our own judgement, anxiety, resentment, and hatred.

Accordingly, we can come to peace from two directions: we can actually change the emotional field around our hearts and thus alter our perceptions; and we can delay automatic responses to perceptions which don't serve our purpose.

We are at a juncture in our evolution. We have developed the capacity to control the impulses, assess feeling and thinking, and make choices appropriate to the situation at hand. We need to practice techniques which will help us choose responses which will be good for us, improve our relations with others, deal with obstacles and crises, help us live more fully in the present, and deepen a sense of meaning in our lives.

When listeners focus on creating a safe environment, on compassion, empathy, and love, the field is determined by those intentions. The process of Compassionate Listening requires an open heart and a focussed mind. One's heart is open to find what connects and to accept and even love the other person, regardless of one's position. The mind is focussed on looking for new possibilities. The following account of a session between Israeli Jews and Arabs is one illustration of the impact this listening can have, and what makes it so compelling.

Though they live in the same city , Jerusalem, they were unlikely to meet under normal circumstances. One is a great grandmother, an Israeli Jew, the other a young, Palestinian, Christian woman. They have come together to participate in a Compassionate Listening training held in a school just outside Bethlehem in the West Bank. This has not been easy for either of them. Ester has entered into Palestinian-controlled territory, which for most Jews is a frightening experience. Mary has never really spoken to Jews before and is holding a great deal of fear. Nevertheless, they have chosen to come and they accept the invitation to tell their stories to the group of trainees.

Ester speaks first. She tells us of the separation from her parents as a young girl in Germany. She was sent to England to escape the Holocaust. Her parents were not as fortunate. Her entire family was killed in Auschwitz. As a young woman, after the war, she ultimately made her way alone to Israel to build a life for herself. Ester told us of her marriage, raising children and the persistence it took, as a woman and mother, to gain an education. She just kept taking classes and eventually earned a degree and recognition for excellence. She spoke of the difficulties of having sons and grandsons serve in the military and the effect it had on their lives. When asked from where her courage came, she recounted the letters her mother had written to her in England and how they imparted the important things about life that a mother wants to pass on to her children. They sustained Ester in her youth and affected her deeply as an adult. She has published a book of these letters.

Then it was Mary's turn to speak. She told us what it was like growing up as a young Palestinian in an occupied territory — the eastern part of Jerusalem. She had lost schoolmates, one shot while riding his bike. She recalled an incident of terror when she was surrounded by Israeli soldiers on her way home from school. She was alone with no one around and was terrified of being dragged away without her family knowing. She spoke of harassment and humiliation. Her fear was evident in her trembling voice throughout her story.

When the two women were finished, the group sat silently for a moment, taking in the tragedy and heroism we had just heard. Immediately, Ester, who had been sitting on the other side of the circle from Mary, came across the room and embraced Mary as a grandmother would her granddaughter, rocking her gently and soothing her.

The lives of Ester and Mary, as well as those of everyone who was a witness, will never be the same again. What we had witnessed was an opening of hearts, the courage to be vulnerable, and the joining together through the common experience of pain and suffering. We saw strength.

Ester and Mary promised to see each other again. Recently, Ester wrote us, "As I told you I have many visitors from Germany. A couple of them I took along yesterday when I went to see Mary at her place of work at the convent. She showed us around and then we sat and talked. She confirmed once more that until the seminar she had never talked to nor touched an Israeli. We had spoken a couple of times by phone to each other, but you should have seen the spark in her eyes when we met again face to face. It was as if we had known each other for a long time. She promised to visit me at home before long."

When asked about Compassionate Listening and what good it can possibly do when the problems in the world are so pervasive, I return in my mind to the many people whose stories I have heard. I am certain, though we may not be able to visibly change the events of the world, that changing one life makes the effort worthwhile. I know lives are altered by these experiences. I am confident compassion and understanding ultimately change the lives of all who participate.

This guidebook has been written to answer the many requests for more information about Compassionate Listening. What is it? Why do we do it? What are its applications? When is it appropriate and when is it not? How do we do it? How could someone become involved? The book has been organized around these questions.

Part One gives the philosophy and theory of Compassionate Listening and what the benefits, results, and outcomes can be.

Part Two introduces the practice. Starting with basic individual preparation through inner work, one learns the basic practical steps for mastering the skills. The chapter, *Individual Preparation*, offers exercises for practice and the mastery of skills for the next step: practicing with other people. Encountering challenges is also addressed in this section. Chapter 6 offers ways to become more involved. It includes exercises and skill-building for working with study groups, projects, and the broader community.

Part Three describes examples of seven different applications of Compassionate Listening Projects now in existence, with contact information.

The **Appendix** section, *Additional Exercises,* provides further material with which to deepen your experience both individually and in group settings.

A Glossary of Terms defines some of the major concepts used in the Compassionate Listening context.

The **Reference** section includes a bibliography and contact information of some groups doing compatible work.

The book was written with the belief that this work should expand and become the basis of all dialogue, whether a Compassionate Listening project, or any other communication. It serves as an invitation to enlarge the community of people, world wide, who know the importance of respect and compassion in all human interactions. It is meant to be both inspirational and practical.

All proceeds from the sale of this *Guidebook* go to The Compassionate Listening Project.

PART ONE:
WHAT COMPASSIONATE LISTENING IS

*I think nonviolence is not
so much a tactic as a way of experiencing
the world within yourself, of understanding the sacred
connection with all of life.
It's an understanding of how everything is
interconnected and how everything is in a
continuing state of relationship.*

Brian Wilson

CHAPTER   1

A PRACTICE REQUIRING INTENTION AND DISCIPLINE

Compassion begins with the acceptance of
what is most human in ourselves, what is most capable of suffering.
In attending to our own capacity to suffer, we can uncover a simple and profound connection
between our own vulnerability and the vulnerability in all others.
Experiencing this allows us to find an instinctive kindness
toward life which is the foundation of all compassion and genuine service.

Rachel Naomi Remen, M.D.

Compassionate Listening is a quality of listening which creates a safe container for people to be free to express themselves and to go to the level of their deep concerns. It simply and profoundly means empathizing with the feelings and condition of people who have been affected by events and circumstances, sometimes of their own doing, and sometimes out of their control. It has everything to do with caring for the state of another human being.

It does not mean agreeing with the position of another person. It does mean putting your own position aside for the moment. It does not imply accepting the blame for something. It does mean listening deeply to the needs and suffering of others and respecting their rights to their opinions. It means putting away advocacy during the trust building.

Compassionate Listening is a dynamic process. It is essential to any dialogue which hopes to lead to peace and possible reconciliation. It enables dialogue and provides the basis of all meaningful relationships. Compassionate Listening groups come together specifically to listen with openness to people who are suffering and are in conflict.

Listening compassionately is a deeply personal process. It is difficult to listen to the opinions of others when in disagreement. It requires impartiality, at least for the moment. We must put our own opinions and judgements aside and pay attention to the human being in whose presence we sit.

This process of listening can be heartbreaking as well as uplifting. We are stretching our capacity to be present and to include pain without making it our own. This becomes a gift through recognizing the possibilities embedded in each event. Through the words, we often witness great strength and courage in the midst of suffering which, through that recognition, is reflected back to its source. Often people feel empowered by listening to themselves.

Listening compassionately is not limited to formal groups and delegations. It is something which can be practiced in all relationships. It is most challenging to listen in the midst of conflict and emotional intensity, especially when it is our own. It is the basis of what may become sustained dialogue. Successful dialogue can only take place when people are ready to really listen to each other and themselves. Dialogue then becomes the basis for problem solving and, ultimately, for advocacy.

Though there are skills we can learn, this practice essentially becomes a personal commitment requiring intention and discipline.

PRACTICE

Compassionate Listening can become a spiritual practice. We touch Spirit when we realize the sacredness in what we are experiencing. When we look at a flower and can really see the magic of the form and color and the tenuousness of its place in the universe, we have touched Spirit. When we hold a rock and can realize this rock is billions of years old and its source is the same as ours: the original stuff of the universe, we have touched Spirit.

When we are sitting in a room, listening to someone with whom we staunchly disagree on deep issues, and when we can reach beyond those issues to the real humanity of that person and connect with the ineffable, we become one. We have touched Spirit. We both are transformed by that process. This is Spirituality.

The practice is first cultivating compassion for our judgements and condemnations which leave us reactive or closed down. This requires self awareness. There are times when our own feelings prevent us from hearing what the other person has said. In this case, using a centering practice helps to keep us neutral.

Traditionally, people have used prayer, meditation, yoga, drumming, and chanting, to name a few, to center themselves. Since anger has a strong physical component, various physical exercises are also appropriate. More recently, we have learned about the heart and its energy impulses, so that energy focusing techniques are also useful. In some parts of the world where energy is better understood, these practices have been used for centuries. Practice develops sensitive listening — listening deeply to ourselves and others in an effort to touch the spirit within.

INTENTION

Creating the ability to listen and encouraging others to do so, requires intention. Our purpose is to resolve conflicts in a peaceful way. We see the need to respect our adversaries, knowing they too have a point of view which is valid for them. This intention is to use skills to manage conflict and achieve outcomes that bring us together rather than separate us. It is not easy. We become warriors of a different kind. We are not battling others. We are battling the forces within us which defend our narrow own self-interests at the expense of considering the greater whole which ultimately benefits us all. Open-hearted intention creates a field for healing to take place.

We interact in such a way that there are only "winners and losers." Ultimately, all must become winners because a win/lose is really a lose/lose. The loser will ultimately seek to regain power and the conflict recycles.

DISCIPLINE

Discipline is interconnected with intention. Intention is not action. It takes discipline to practice these skills so they will become second nature. People have developed many practices which help to delay the immediate emotional response to conflict. They all seem to have one thing in common: that of centering oneself, engaging the heart, and paying attention to the greater whole.

The deepest level of communication is not communication but communion. It is wordless. It is beyond words and beyond speech, and it is beyond concept. Not that we discover a new unity. We discover an older unity. We are already one, but we imagine that we are not. And what we have to recover is our original unity. What we have to be is what we are.

Thomas Merton, Speech in Calcutta

CHAPTER 2

BENEFITS, RESULTS, AND OUTCOMES

An eye for an eye and we all go blind.
M. Gandhi

A human being is part of the whole called by us a 'universe,'

a part limited in time and space. We experience ourselves, our thoughts and feelings

as something separate from the rest — a kind of optical delusion of consciousness.

This delusion is a kind of prison for us, restricting us to our personal desires and to affection for a

few persons nearest to us. Our task must be to free ourselves from this prison by widening our circle of compassion

to embrace all living creatures and the whole of nature in its beauty.
Albert Einstein

CREATES MEANING

Meaning is a form of strength. It has the power to transform experience, to open the most difficult of work to the dimension of joy and even gratitude. Meaning is the language of the soul. Few works of service can endure unless they are sustained by a lifted sense of their meaning and purpose.

Rachel Naomi Remen, M.D.

Our world is a complex and chaotic system. The issues we face are large and difficult to solve because we all hold little pieces of the solutions, and we don't get the whole picture. The work to be done is connecting the pieces we do recognize into manageable yet ever increasing levels of complexity in order to uncover meaning. We live in an information age and find problems overwhelming because it is difficult to organize complex information into meaningful units. Linking ideas and networking with people is pivotal at this juncture in time. Inclusion is essential.

In the case of conflict, all parties to the conflict hold elements of the solution and need to be heard. Listening to a divergent view can even

clarify one's own view. Astute listening can detect elements of agreement in divergent positions. The opening of one's heart allows one to stay present and connected to listen for these elements. The connection allows for a glimpse of the greater whole, wherein lies the solution. When we all offer our piece of the puzzle, the picture emerges.

A major principle of Quantum Physics is: the whole is greater than the sum of its parts. One can dismantle a clock and have an impressive array of pieces. However, only until they are assembled in a way that they connect and interact with each other, will they function as a clock. This principle has social implications, as well. People going their separate ways cannot even provide for their basic needs effectively without group effort. Everything we do is interrelated. When we collaborate with a common goal, we can overcome obstacles we could never surmount alone. Compassionate Listening is the key to this collaboration. Meaning is embedded in the message.

Positions and opinions are but the tip of the iceberg. They represent other levels of deeper and broader concern. While listening compassionately, we are understanding conflict at other levels. Einstein cautioned that a problem cannot be solved at the level it was created. In relationships, we need to be looking for the areas where the components come together to create new perspectives. Simultaneously, we are listening for the "deeper" needs. Humans beings are more alike than not. Our deeper needs are basic to all: safety, food, belonging, love, social approval, self approval and self actualization, as identified by Abraham Maslow. Every human has a need to be seen and acknowledged.

There is a distinct difference between judging another and disagreeing with his/her position. Our judgements condemn the person with whom we disagree. Disagreement, in itself is not harmful. We need to understand our disagreements and positions in order to find solutions which are beneficial to us all. Though there are times when we need to listen for detail within a position, Compassionate Listening is not about finding agreement on positions. It is about uncovering the deeper, unexpressed interests, needs, and concerns which are the basis of positions. This sensitive listening sets out to uncover those commonalities.

Since we each see only a part of reality, learning to see more requires that we take in other points of view and learn to work with them. No matter how minutely we examine positions, parts, pieces, data, individual aspects, we will not understand the whole and what meaning it holds. Listening to divergent positions helps to broaden perspectives and understand a greater picture.

We live in a "chaordic" time – a word developed by Dee Hock in his book, *Birth of the Chaordic Age*. When one looks at the problems of the world, they seem insurmountable in their complexity. We live in an information age where we know more about the challenges which face the whole planet than ever before. The full impact of our interconnection must be comprehended for our survival. All these bits of information present themselves as chaotic. And yet we know that at some level there is an order. How do we find solutions for issues of such magnitude?

One need only to look at political systems as they now function in many countries. It is only a matter of time before the weaker one regains power and the struggle continues and escalates. Conflicts are spinning out of control and people often feel hopeless. The power struggle is part of a dysfunctional paradigm. We see signs it is being replaced, slowly as it may seem, by a new way of interaction.

Compassionate listening skills offer a means for finding answers – even large ones. Since we are all part of the problem, we are all part of the solution. We need to approach those who hold divergent points of view - even our enemies. All points of view need to be factored into solutions in order for them to work. Each person has a part of the answer. We must listen to each other. We must hold compassion for those with whom we differ, put our hatred aside and get to work.

I had invited a young environmental activist to participate in a Compassionate Listening workshop I was teaching. She declined as she was going to be in the forest teaching activists how to resist the loggers in their attempts to cut the trees. As is true in many communities, environmentalists and industrial advocates are literally at war – a war focussed on demonstrations and in the courts. Huge amounts of time, energy and resources are spent on this war. I have found, in talking to both sides, that often, though not always, the concerns are similar. There is common ground from which solutions can be developed. How can acceptable solutions be found if groups won't talk to each other? What are the basic, underlying needs of all parties? Where is the common ground? What mutually acceptable solutions can be generated from this common ground? Compassionate Listening has an important role to play in finding the order which is embedded in the chaos. It is the first step for strategic problem solving. It is a decided form of activism. It is an appropriate step for transforming all conflict.

EMPOWERS THE INDIVIDUAL

When we are listened to, it creates us, makes us unfold and expand. Ideas actually begin to grow within us and come to life.

Brenda Ueland

Compassionate Listening is a deeply personal process which is applicable to every facet of life, from deeply internal conflicts to all relationships. People feel empowered when using these skills, because they see results. Often we feel at a loss, not knowing what to do in an adversarial situation. When people learn and practice these skills of listening, they change themselves. Everyone can do this. In the training programs I have taught, seemingly to solve conflicts between family members, organizations and ethnic groups, the real benefit is that deep personal changes occur. People report they feel personally empowered, for they have developed tools of listening which not only are effective with their own internal conflicts, but with personal and work relationships as well. Listening is a powerful tool for the listener as well as the one listened to.

In a conflict resolution class I was teaching, a seventh grader reported she had used the process of mediation with her parents, who had been in conflict the preceding night. She had interrupted their argument and offered an alternative. The child took on the role of mediator and listened, having her parents join her in looking for the underlying needs and interests. This child felt empowered to intervene because she had learned new skills.

RESOLVES CONFLICT

I changed. I learned something about compassionate listening. I felt that the very thing that had separated us felt like the point of connection. I continued to experience that with other people. If I could listen and drop down inside to a quiet level of experience, I could find their wound inside me. I felt like we were part of something larger.

Susan Heckler, MECD Delegate

Listening is the major component to all conflict resolution. The role of a mediator is to encourage communication between parties and to listen for possibilities of cooperation and agreement. When a mediator is not present, and we ourselves are engaged in a conflict, we can draw upon the "mediator within." This is a term for the awareness which allows us to put our own positions aside for a time and engage in deep empathic listening to the other side.

Reflecting back or restating the essence of what you heard the other person say, clarifies that person's position and can also bring forth the underlying issues. Next, you can ask the other person to listen to your side and clarify your position and underlying issues. By that time, there is a feeling of mutuality and finding agreement can proceed more easily. We don't have to depend upon others to guide us through empathic listening, even when we are in the heat of our own conflicts. We can initiate the process ourselves, thus empowering all parties.

Too often we focus on finding solutions to problems without searching for clarity at the deepest level of the problem. The reason conflict recycles is that the underlying interests, needs and concerns have not been addressed. Resolution has been based on a compromise of positions which might make it seem an agreement has been reached. But unless those underlying levels are satisfied, the cycle of conflict will continue, albeit, sometimes in a different form. In conflict, stated positions mistakenly become the focus of attention. There are underlying interests, needs and concerns attached to each position. Listening for and identifying those broader interests expands the possibility for mutuality. When agreement can be found at those levels, resolution is at hand.

This is evident in a family conflict. The parties might agree on a new way to solve issues, but often the peace does not hold and conflict breaks out again in a different form. The deeper relationship issues and areas of discontent must be addressed, which can then lead to resolution.

HEALS DEEP WOUNDS

*To reconcile conflicting parties, we must
have the ability to understand the suffering
of both sides. If we take sides, it is impos-
sible to do the work of reconciliation. And
human beings want to take sides. That is
why the situation gets worse and worse.
Are there people who are still available to
both sides? They need not do much. They
need only do one thing: go to one side and
tell all about the suffering endured by the
other side, and go to the other side and tell
all about the suffering endured by this side.
That is our chance for peace. That can
change the situation. But how many of us
are able to do that?*

Thich Nhat Hanh

In searching for clarity at deeper levels, we listen
to the grievances of each side and communicate
them to the other, including the feelings of
suffering. Suffering is a common denominator.
When all parties recognize their own suffering
and can acknowledge the suffering they have
inflicted, the process of true reconciliation
proceeds. This is not an easy process and takes a
significant amount of inner strength to acknowledge the suffering one might have inflicted or
one's group might have inflicted on another.

This process does not mean taking blame. An
action might well have been justified. It means
acknowledgement and sorrow for the suffering
which resulted. Actually, this level of vulnerability is truly empowering.

Sessions do not become a contest between
which side has suffered the most. When we
really listen to the suffering of others, our hearts
open and competition and conflict dissolve.
From this level of mutual suffering, people can
gently build relationship from a level of trust.

I counseled a woman who had been sexually
abused as a child by a family member. For twenty-
five years, the whole family denied that this had
happened. Her healing began when the perpetrator finally admitted what he had done and apolo-
gized for his behavior. He couldn't undo it, but he
could acknowledge her pain and suffering.

Not only does listening compassionately deepen
our understanding of ourselves, other people
and situations, it can diffuse conflict and heal
deep emotional wounds. It changes lives of those
listened to and the lives of the listeners, as well.
Conflict can lead to transformation and healing.

*"Whether you're in conversation with
doctors, healers, friends, yourself or God,
the sacred art of listening is an extraordinary resource for your healing. Being
diagnosed with a life threatening illness
challenges any philosophic ideas you may
have about mind/body healing. Listening,
really listening, nurtures and guides you to
make choices for your body and your life
which are an authentic expression of who
you are."*

Amy Schnapper

CONTRIBUTES TO A CIVIL SOCIETY

*What have I ever done in 50 years that
would make you burn my house?*

Dervis Audaja, to his Serb
neighbors as he fled Kosovo,
Life Magazine, 1/00

Citizen efforts are incredibly important in enact-
ing peace in a civil society. Listening is not only a
key component to resolving conflicts, but is also
effective in preventing conflicts. Compassionate
Listening seeks to establish relationship through
deep listening with the heart. By contrast,
politicians work with positions, a mental approach. Both approaches are necessary for
peace and a functioning society.

In almost all the areas of dissention around the
globe at this time, warfare has erupted between
people who have been living cooperatively sometimes for centuries. National borders have shifted
many times because of colonialism and wars.
Ethnic groups have been divided, yet in many
cases, they have lived together multi-ethnically
quite peaceably. When leadership begins to fan the
flames of discontent, as in the case of the former
Yugoslavia, explosion results: and we have recently
witnessed this in many parts of the world. Listening and conflict resolution need to be reinforced on

every level of every society as the first choice before civil dissention arises.

Governments cannot make peace work through treaties and border changes. It's even difficult for governments to wage war without civilian cooperation. People who understand the principles of compassionate listening — listening for solutions hidden within the hearts of all involved — these people are going to find ways to cooperate and solve civil problems. Unless peace is generated among the people who live it out, treaties are not really operational on a practical level. It is the plain ordinary person who ultimately lives peace or not. We need to build opportunities in all communities for people to listen to each other.

"I strongly believe that people have to keep talking to each other, or perhaps better said, have to learn to talk to each other no matter what the political situation. I know that that is not easy, but that is where Compassionate Listening comes in.

"Last Thursday I participated with the Women in Black at the demonstration in Jerusalem. As has been reported, a group of Kach rightists began to mingle with us, calling out taunting remarks and setting up their signs alongside us. The police had not yet arrived. So I decided to communicate my interest in Listening, not arguing, to two of the rightists at different times. These were fairly brief contacts, during which each of the two men toned down their voices and agreed or suggested that we move off to the side where it was quieter. Soon, of course, the leaders told them strongly to get back to their group, although in each case they tried to stay and continue talking.

"My point is that in each case, they asked me: 'Why don't you people talk also with us, and not only with the Arabs?' That started me wondering: how much has the peace movement tried listening to the rightists? I know of lots of dialogue initiatives, but of course I am talking about real Compassionate Listening."

Bracha Yanov

Many indigenous societies have had structures in place. The democracy of the United States is partially based on such principles of the Iroquois Nation, implemented by Thomas Jefferson and Benjamin Franklin. Our nation has benefitted from what we learned from First Nation peoples, but tragically has not applied these principles in our interactions with our indigenous population.

"Sulha" is the traditional Arabic form of reconciliation which brings conflicting parties together to address the wrong while saving face, and to create relationship. Since conflict is a part of life, every culture has had a traditional way of mitigating it. They are based on compassionate listening.

BABEMBA JUSTICE

In the Babemba tribe in South Africa, when a person acts irresponsibly or unjustly, he is placed in the center of the village, alone and unfettered.

All work ceases, and every man, woman and child in the village gathers in a large circle around the accused individual.

Then each person in the tribe, regardless of age, begins to talk out loud to the accused, one at a time, about all the good things the person in the center of the circle has done in his lifetime.

Every incident, every experience that can be recalled with any detail and accuracy is recounted.

All his positive attributes, good deeds, strengths and kindnesses are recited carefully and at length. No one is permitted to fabricate, exaggerate or be facetious about his accomplishments or the positive aspects of his personality.

The tribal ceremony often lasts several days and does not cease until everyone is drained of every positive comment he or she can state about the person in question.

At the end, the tribal circle is broken, a joyous celebration takes place, and the person symbolically and literally is welcomed back into the tribe.

Fortunately, there are projects too numerous to list which give hope for the future in many parts of the world. And there are acts of compassion and courage on the part of individuals everywhere which may lead one to believe that peacemaking may become more natural to humans than fighting.

LEADS TO FORGIVENESS AND POSSIBLE RECONCILIATION

The inner peace and security we long for is found first and foremost in forgiveness.

Yehezkel Landau

It isn't easy, as we all know, to ask for forgiveness and it's also not easy to forgive, but we are people who know that when someone cannot be forgiven there is no future.

Desmond Mpilo Tutu

For some, forgiveness means dropping the desire for revenge and resolving not to initiate harm toward the other. Some people are able to forgive the person, but not the deed, and continue to insist on rightful punishment. Justice is a very important part of the restorative process of which forgiveness is but a step.

Forgiveness can occur without reconciliation or the resumption of relationship. In many cases, people are no longer available for a relationship because of proximity or death, or being unknown. We may never be able to have, or even want a direct relationship with someone we feel has harmed us. Yet one can be free from the chains of hatred by working internally through the steps of forgiveness. This provides the ultimate freedom to not be bound by another, but choosing to be unburdened from resentment.

A former inmate of a Nazi concentration camp was visiting a friend who had shared the ordeal with him.

'Have you forgiven the Nazis?', he asked his friend.

'Yes.'

'Well, I haven't. I'm still consumed with hatred for them.'

'In that case,' said his friend gently, 'They still have you prisoner.'

Ernest Kurtz and Katharine Kitcham

Forgiveness means different things to different people. It is both culturally and religiously formed. When I attended a seminar on forgiveness and reconciliation attended by people from many diverse cultures and countries where wars have been festering, I was amazed to hear the different interpretations of the word "forgiveness." I became aware of how in the United States, the general meaning of the word means to "turn the other cheek." I realized how the meaning is in a Christian context. For many of the seminar participants, this was totally unacceptable. What bothers many people about the "turning the other cheek" approach is that often they do not want to resume a relationship where they have been harmed.

In Jerusalem, we listened to an Israeli psychiatrist who facilitates a support group for Israelis who have been wounded by terrorist activities. He knows first hand of what he speaks since he, too, has been wounded by a terrorist bomb. He spoke to us about forgiveness and reconciliation and how it is first an internal process. One has to work through the emotional and psychological effect of the event. Forgiveness comes from acceptance of the damage. From that acceptance comes self empowerment, which is not dependent upon the perpetrator. The victim is free to recover autonomy and independence through this acceptance without reconciliation. He spoke of how people become trapped in trying to grasp why something happens. Understanding may or may not ever happen. But autonomy and empowerment can happen independently of understanding.

Forgiveness is to relinquish your grievance and so to let go of grief.

Eckhart Tolle

10

In a seminar many years ago, working with adolescents who had behavior problems, I was struck by a major point the instructor made. "A person," she said, "has always done the best s/he could with the resources available at that moment in time, or they would have done it differently." That statement didn't sit well with me for a long time. Slowly, I began to realize, that for me, the truth of that statement was the basis of the meaning of forgiveness. It meant people do the best they can in the moment with what resources they have. This doesn't mean what they did was right, just, or even conscionable. They made one choice and not another for some underlying reason. I had to begin looking deeply at the meaning of blame and responsibility. Even what appears to be an irresponsible behavior still makes sense to that person at that time. When I really understood this, it became easier to disapprove of the behavior, yet forgive and even love the person. It provided a way of keeping a connection with someone whose behavior I could not condone. The re-establishment of relationship — reconciliation — is the ideal outcome of forgiveness.

ENCOURAGES STORIES

Story is our nearest and dearest way of our understanding our lives and finding our way onward.

Ursula Le Guin

We have lost many treasures with the fast pace of life — a notable one is the listening to peoples' stories. Traditionally, stories have served as the glue for the culture — the clan, the family, and the nation. Through stories our ethics, values and traditions have not only been relayed verbally, but also modeled through the telling. Embedded in each story is a clue which can help to unravel the mystery of human nature. What possibly could have led this person to believe what s/he believes?

Stories serve as a walk through time and place by relating the past and revealing the present which will become history with the telling. History comes alive. Events take on a deeply personal tone and one enters into another dimension of reality. History becomes understandable on a human level and other pieces of the unknown puzzle are revealed.

There is a larger story in the telling. When the story teller is emotionally connected to the story, strength is revealed. It takes incredible courage to remain vulnerable. It is not a performance. We enter into a sacred space. It is life making itself known through this person. We hear ourselves in another's story for we are more alike than not. The story line may describe different events, but the experiences of each life touch the same emotions in us all. We can relate. Encouraging people to tell their stories is a way to make basic human connection. Stories are heard by both the listener and the teller. When we tell our story, we hear ourselves and what is important to us. We love and are loved and can appreciate the fears of loss we all share. Acknowledging these fears, griefs, and joys builds connection and trust. We are seen.

Stories show us what it is like to be human, sometimes showing us the heights of the human spirit in overcoming adversity. We witness what Joseph Campbell referred to as the "heroic journey," which ultimately leads to the transformation of hatred and pain to the power of love. It is difficult to hear the toll certain events have had on individuals and to witness their suffering. The ugly events of history become personal and real and their emotional impact cannot be erased.

My most challenging listening was during a parole hearing for the murderer of my niece some years ago. As he presented his case and told his story, I was occupied listening between the lines to his tragic life, to the attitudes which led to this devastating event. I could not condone the act, yet ultimately, I could hold empathy for him. His story touched my heart.

The real challenge of Compassionate Listening is to hear the stories of both the oppressed and the oppressors, to listen to people who hold very different values from our own, and to develop empathy for the human being which transcends the issues.

PART TWO:
HOW TO PRACTICE IT

The art of creating understanding is
like weaving a fabric from the many threads of silence,
timing, inflection, intent, and other non-verbal cues.
It requires a delicate balance between assertiveness and
receptivity. Listening is at the core.

Carol Hwoschinsky

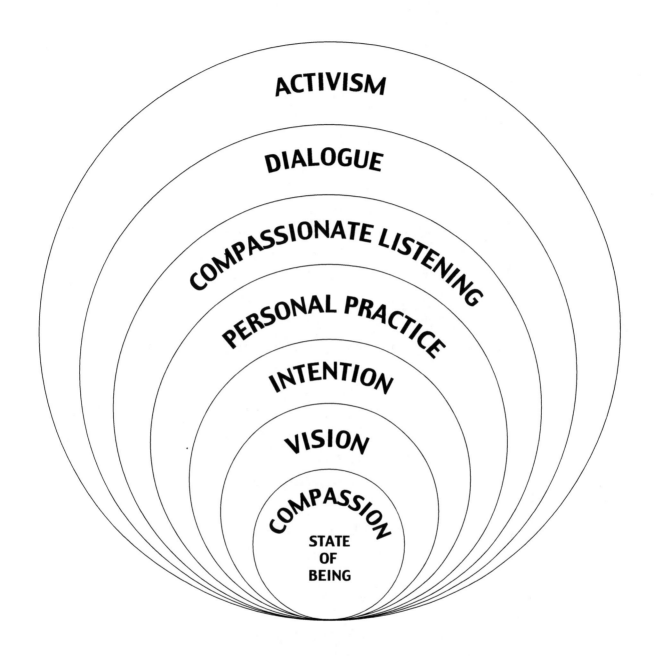

ACTIVISM

DIALOGUE

COMPASSIONATE LISTENING

PERSONAL PRACTICE

INTENTION

VISION

COMPASSION

STATE
OF
BEING

**COMPASSIONATE LISTENING
PRACTICE**

PLEASE CALL ME BY MY TRUE NAMES

Don't say that I will depart tomorrow —
even today I am still arriving.

Look deeply: every second I am arriving
to be a bud on a Spring branch,
to be a tiny bird, with still-fragile wings,
learning to sing in my new nest,
to be a caterpillar in the heart of a flower,
to be a jewel hiding itself in a stone.

I still arrive, in order to laugh and to cry,
to fear and to hope.
The rhythm of my heart is the birth and death
of all that is alive.

I am a mayfly metamorphosing
on the surface of the river.
And I am the bird
that swoops down to swallow the mayfly.

I am a frog swimming happily
in the clear water of a pond.
And I am the grass-snake
that silently feeds itself on the frog.

I am the child in Uganda,
all skin and bones,
my legs as thin as bamboo sticks.
And I am the arms merchant,
selling deadly weapons to Uganda.

I am the twelve-year-old girl,
refugee on a small boat,
who throws herself into the ocean
after being raped by a sea pirate.
And I am the pirate,
my heart not yet capable
of seeing and loving.

I am a member of the politburo,
with plenty of power in my hands.
And I am the man who has to pay
his "debt of blood" to my people
dying slowly in a forced-labor camp.

My joy is like Spring, so warm
it makes flowers bloom all over the Earth.
My pain is like a river of tears,
so vast it fills the four oceans.

Please call me by my true names,
so I can hear all my cries and laughter at once,
so I can see that my joy and pain are one.

Please call me by my true names,
so I can wake up
and the door of my heart
could be left open,
the door of compassion.

Thich Nhat Hanh

This poem was written in 1978, during the time of helping the boat people. It was first read at a retreat in Kosmos Center in Amsterdam, Holland, organized by Niko Tidman.

Reprinted from: *Call Me by My True Names: The Collected Poems of Thich Nhat Hanh* (1999) by Thich Nhat Hanh with permission of Parallax Press, Berkeley, CA

C H A P T E R   3

INDIVIDUAL PREPARATION

As human beings,

our greatness lies not so much in being able to remake the world —

that is the myth of the 'atomic age'— as in being able to remake ourselves.

Mahatma Gandhi

The basic components of preparation consist of a fundamental understanding of the principles of Compassionate Listening (CL); what it is and what it isn't; and when it is used. This theoretical material has been covered in *Part One, What Compassionate Listening Is.*

In *Part Two, How To Practice It,* you will find the preparation necessary for you to pursue any of a number of outcomes. It offers exercises, processes, considerations, and skill building for the basic practice of CL. Further exercises are given in *Additional Exercises* at the end of the book. *Chapter 3* covers basic individual preparation and exercises for individual practice, the foundation for all CL involvement. Some people may want to develop a personal practice and not take this work beyond that. For those who do wish to prepare for group involvement, *Part Three, How to be Involved*, continues with those progressive steps.

The unexamined life is not worth living.

Socrates

Individual preparation involves, primarily, learning to come to presence — to bring attention to the "now" — not pulled away by internal judgements and conflicts, nor distracted by ideas and events in the environment. Being quiet internally and attentive leads us to be fully present to another person.

The work means clearing the concerns we have with the people and issues which are close to us. Come to terms with what we don't like. Be integrous with the way we deal with what upsets us. Bring attention and softening to our passions and our aversions. It does not mean being neutral about life but directing the energy of our lives with integrity.

Develop a plan for your personal practice. Choose exercises which fit the plan. Start listening to the issues of the people right around you: the grocery clerk, the airline ticketer, the doctor's receptionist. Listen consciously and compassionately to members of your family. Identify the places in your life where compassionate listening is relatively easy for you and pay attention to how you engage. Then move into more and more difficult areas, noticing your responses and reactions to people and issues. What are the difficult areas for you and why are they difficult? Can you practice putting your own opinions aside while you listen? What are the inner conflicts which arise? Are there particular people who "push your buttons?" Take a look at those buttons. What makes it so difficult to put them aside to listen?

Cynthia Monroe, of Alaskans Listening to Alaskans about Subsistence, cautions us to not get involved in situations which are too difficult for us.

"You must not try to take on the Compassionate Listening role in any public way around an issue where your own experience is too fresh or painful. You will get hurt, and you will hurt those with whom you set out to build bridges. If you feel in your heart that a certain person or group is unreachable, evil, or beyond hope, do not become involved in compassionate listening with that group or individual. If you are already involved, and find you feel this way, excuse yourself from the situation, or from the project.

It is perfectly all right to feel this way, and vitally important to recognize when you do. It may mean you need to rest and come back to it later, or it may mean that the work you are called to with this particular issue is not compassionate listening, but more direct activism."

Bring healing to the areas which are difficult for you by becoming aware of inner conflicts, practicing centering and working with the shadow parts of yourself.

PERSONAL VISION

Have no expectations, but hold abundant expectancy.

Diane Pike and Arlene Lorrance
of The Love Project

Our vision is what motivates and guides us. We are attracted to this work because we have a vision of a more peaceful world. The qualities of this vision actually unleash an energy which moves us toward a desired goal. To touch in with this sense of purpose is both humbling and empowering. It is humbling to imagine we can create a peaceful world by our own personal involvement. However, when people join together around a shared vision, the force is powerful. It gives coherence to otherwise diverse activities.

CONNECTING WITH YOUR VISION

It is helpful to ask the questions during a relaxed, meditative state. Some people respond better to images and symbols rather than words. After this initial receptive questioning, I advise the vision be written and/or drawn, and verbalized to others who now have an opportunity to practice compassionate listening for you.

Questions to consider are:

How did I come by this interest (passion) in Compassionate Listening? Why am I here? What have been the steps throughout my life which have led me to this place at this time?

What areas of this field excite me? Where am I now on this journey? Where am I going with it? Is there anything which gets in the way of my manifesting my highest vision? What resources do I have within myself and beyond myself to work through these obstacles? Who are the people who serve as inspiration and as guides? How do I join with others?

DEEPENING QUESTIONS

Gene Knudsen Hoffman presents quotes with questions designed to deepen our understanding of our own responses to compassion, denial, forgiveness, and reconciliation. This is an example of her introduction to her section entitled Compassion. The full text can be downloaded from her website <coopcomm.org>,

"We must love them both, those whose opinions we share, and those whose opinions we reject, for both have labored in the search for truth, and both have helped in the finding of it."
Thomas Aquinas

• How can we feel compassion for those whose opinions we reject, particularly if their opinions propose violence against people?
• What are the steps we can take to show them we 'love' them?
• How have they both labored in the search for truth? How has our opposition helped us in the finding of it?
• What is so important about searching for truth? What do we think truth is?

- Have you ever loved someone with whom you totally disagreed? How was it? How did you handle it? Discuss your answers.

INNER CONFLICTS

For many of us, our internal landscape is like a war zone. This is a common obstacle to listening compassionately in a conflict situation. Within us are many voices, resistant to listening, and often in conflict with one another. I am referring to our own judgements and condemnations which are apt to distract us from our intention to be unbiased and listen compassionately. When these biases remain hidden from our awareness, we refer to them as "shadow." The danger of shadow is that of projecting on to someone else the characteristics we don't see in ourselves. This is how an enemy is made. For example, if we deny judgement in ourselves, we might see other people as holding judgement. Judgement is a common shadow.

However, being judgmental about our own judgements doesn't work for the exact same reasons it doesn't work when we're judgmental of others. Judgement energizes resistance. Empathy neutralizes. Trying to get rid of something only makes it stronger. It is best to come to terms with this cacophony of inner voices, bringing them to a place of awareness and showing compassion for ourselves. This is a human condition and we are not exempt. We can see how being non-judgmental toward another person dissipates their resistance. This works equally within ourselves. Bringing compassion to that which we dislike in ourselves is the only way to de-energize our resistances. All of our repetitive attitudes and behaviors are there because they have helped us adapt to events in our past. They have protected us and have worked for us in some way or we wouldn't still be relying on them.

The events of the past are no longer with us and we are more mature and self-empowered than we were when we developed them. These vestiges of our past have become habitual even though they no longer serve us. One way to de-energize them is to identify new ways which are more appropriate for our present situations and plan ways to remember to engage these new responses when we find our selves in the old patterns. It is an ongoing process of self forgiveness.

Noticing inner conflicts often disarms them of their power over us and helps us be more compassionate when we see them in others. Sharing them with a partner often leads to recognition that we are not alone on this path of uncovering the "ghosts in the closet."

CENTERING

Listening to people in conflict, in pain, or who hold different positions from ours, can create stress and distract us from full attention. Sometimes we experience strong emotions ourselves. The body is the indicator of our emotions. Locating where we feel a sensation in the body helps us to identify what the emotion is and helps in its release. Tightness in the chest, a knot in the stomach, sweaty palms and feet, tension in the head and around the eyes, are some of the common indicators of emotional stress. Many people find it difficult to attune to these physical indicators. Most everyone can find some way which can be helpful in releasing stress and coming to a centered state by focusing on the body. Attention to the breath is often used to center the whole being.

Refer to *Additional Exercises* in the *Appendix* for additional material.

CHAPTER FOUR

SKILLS

This listening requires a particular mode.

The questions are non-adversarial. The listening is non-judgmental.

The listener seeks the truth of the person questioned, and strives to see through any

masks of hostility and fear to the sacredness of the individual,

and discerns the wounds at the heart of any violence.

Listeners do not defend themselves,

but accept whatever others say as their perception and validate their right to it.

Gene Knudsen-Hoffman

Having specific skills to practice takes an idea into willful action. At first, some of these skills may feel awkward and insincere. When practicing them individually and in a study group, you will learn to incorporate them into your own style. When this happens, the awkwardness will most likely disappear and the skills will become a sincere expression of your interest and compassion for another person.

INQUIRY

The essential questions have no answers.
You are my question, and I am yours —
and then there is dialogue. The moment
we have answers, there is no dialogue.
Questions unite people, answers divide
them. So why have answers when you can
live without them?

Elie Wiesel

In Compassionate Listening, inquiry can either make or break the safe containment of the process. As listeners, we are asking people to share personal experiences, sometimes of a very vulnerable nature. Knowing how to ask questions is pivotal as to whether a person will shut down or not. The learning is how to ask from the heart in a way that helps understanding and empathy and keeps the ball in the speaker's field.

We need to be aware of the impact certain kinds of questions will have on the speaker because questions can be a way of interrupting the flow, can be inflammatory, can avoid vulnerability, and can be a way of showing off how much you know. When you do make an inquiry, be clear on the intention of the question before asking it. Is it to understand? learn? influence? challenge? camouflage your own opinion? focus attention? guide continued exploration?

Listeners use inquiry in a healing way. The questions can have meaning embedded which can move people out of a stuck place by offering a broader perspective, giving a sense of hope and purpose, and calling upon the best in people. They can imply the possibility for positive outcomes by guiding people to recall past success, explore possibilities, strengthen motivation, and clear distorted perceptions.

The key in formulating questions is to keep them open ended. Offer questions which can not be easily answered with a "yes/no" answer, and allow for a wide range of responses. Keep questions exploratory.

Here are some examples:
Early in the process:
- Can you tell us about the situation that concerns you?
- How has this situation affected your life?

During the process:
- Could you say more about that?
- What was that like for you?
- Could you elaborate on that?
- How do you feel about.......?
- I'm wondering what views others might have about this?
- If this situation were fully resolved, how would things be better for you?
- Help me understand how this is important to you.

More questions to consider which open up possibilities:
- Hope! Are you hopeful?
- What does love mean in your culture? Religion?
- What about forgiveness?
- Disputes reach the levels they do because of deep, unmet needs. What deep, unmet needs to you see at work in this situation?
- Empathy opens the field of possibility to be of service (our highest human need). What is your service?

Questions are to facilitate the process. Often, they are not needed at all. The big caution is not to ask questions to satisfy your own curiosity, but use them to facilitate the process. Put out a question with purpose and then stay out of the way.

REFLECTIVE LISTENING

While all of Compassionate Listening is an active process, there are certain additional techniques of actively responding which are useful to mention.

Inquiry can open up possibilities. Reflective Listening (RL) also encourages expression and clarifies understanding with a statement rather than a question. RL is the restatement of what you have heard a speaker say to you for the purpose of clarification and encouragement. A second stage can be used to clarify a feeling the listener has heard embedded in the message. RL does not denote agreement.

RL is used in the Compassionate Listening environment:
- when we sense we do not fully understand why the person feels or thinks the way s/he does and we would like to learn more about how s/he experiences their situation;
- to verify a feeling the listener has heard embedded in the message;
- when we sense there is more to what the other person is saying than what is being expressed;
- to summarize from time to time in order to pull together important ideas and establish a basis for further discussion.

REFLECTIVE LISTENING PROCESS

Break into triads: one speaker, one listener, one observer
- the speakers talks for 4 minutes about something important to them;
- listener practices reflective listening;
- observer calls time at the end of the four minutes

Process the activity in the small groups for five minutes by having the observers ask questions:

For the speaker:
- How did you feel during your sharing?
- What did the listener do that encouraged you to talk more?
- Did the listener do anything that discouraged you from talking?
- How did you feel at the end of the discussion?

For the listener:
- What made it difficult or easy for you to listen?
- What techniques were easiest or most difficult for you to use?

The observer can give feedback on how effectively the listener used the active listening techniques.

Rotate roles and repeat the exercise until each person has had an opportunity to be in each role.

Questions for the group:
- What are the benefits of using these techniques for the speaker, for the listener?
- What are the drawbacks?

The major point to be made about RL is that it must be sincere and not used as a "technique." We can all remember times when it was used with us and we have felt manipulated. As with all these skills, it's a good idea to know their value, practice them, then let go of the technique and rely on your own judgement and intuition about how and when to use them.

WORKING WITH ANGER

Anger is simply energy and serves as an indicator that something is not right with us. We can learn to listen to it, yet not act on it against ourselves or others. We need to befriend our anger personally and culturally because the results of this unrecognized anger can be destructive. Until we re-own it as an integral part of ourselves — as an emotion we all experience at times — it will pour forth without control. It is the denial of anger which leads to violence. It is a powerful personal and collective shadow. When we uncover this energy of anger and see it for what it is, we find it is a mask for fear. When anger is plumbed, there is a hidden and strong fear lurking. That is where the attention should be paid, therefore dissipating the need to lash out. Accepting anger as an adaptation to fear and an expression of an unmet need, allows us to be more accepting when we experience it in ourselves and others, and to recognize our projections.

EXPLORING EMOTIONS

Taking Charge of Emotions: what are they?
- List those you feel comfortable with and those with which you feel uncomfortable;
- Have a discussion about your physical responses to both the comfortable and uncomfortable lists;
- Discuss how your family of origin dealt with emotions generally;
- What were their fears and expectations?
- What societal expectations were important?
- How have these factors influenced you?
- Can you see the relationship between your unattended emotions and your projections?

CHAPTER 5

ENCOUNTERING CHALLENGES

All humans have the same needs— the requests are different.

Marshal Rosenberg

There are people in this world we consider difficult. Often, the people we consider difficult are so because they hold different values, assumptions and beliefs from what ours may be. If they are difficult for us, we are most likely difficult for them. We do come upon groups and individuals within groups who present themselves as "difficult." They may test the leadership, their behavioral style may be challenging, and they may be disrespectful, by our standards. And sometimes, people use anger as a strategy to intimidate as a way to make their point or to dominate a situation.

We try to remain centered and non judgmental so we can understand the hidden messages. Listening respectfully most often diffuses the intensity.

On one occasion in Israel, we were hosted by a very prestigious Israeli educational institute where we showed the film about our work, *Children of Abraham* to over a hundred Jewish Israelis. After the film, our group of eighteen Americans came forward and stood in the front of the room to answer questions and to listen. The first comments were delivered in the form of a tirade berating us, as Americans, for not knowing what the real situation was. "The problem is you don't live here and experience it as an Israeli experience," said one of the viewers. Others agreed and added their explications. For about fifteen minutes, all the comments were critical.

As I stood there in the company of our delegation, I first felt a knot in my stomach and thought, "How are we going to handle this?" I felt

exposed standing in the front of the room and experienced a wave of shame because I had not pleased these people. After the second comment or so, I remembered my centering practice: feeling my feet planted firmly on the earth and breathing deeply through my belly. That was my way of dealing with the energy being hurled at us by members of the audience.

Our group members responded with dignity and composure, acknowledging the perception of the accusers and standing strongly in their own experience. Delegation members spoke simply of what they personally had seen and learned on this trip. They were eloquent, informative, and totally non-defensive.

The mood of the audience began to calm and they began to acknowledge us and the process. People, who had at first been silent began to comment on the similarities of their perceptions to what they had seen in the film. They thanked us for presenting a part of life which they observed they, themselves, do not have an opportunity to witness. They spoke of the balance of the content of the film and how hard it was to see "the other side." A woman stood up half way through and said, "You know, we Israelis have to admit that listening is a very radical concept in Israel, but I think these people [our delegates] are onto something."

That evening will always stay indelibly in my mind. I was keenly aware of how my centering practice made me more available to be present to the criticism and not to take it personally, but to learn from it. And secondly, I was impressed with how our delegation of people had all responded with such integrity. The listeners lives clearly had been changed by this work. There was actually a great deal of transformation that evening.

STYLES OF RESOLVING CONFLICT

Instead of being caught in a vicious circle, we can start a virtuous circle — not by closing our eyes to hostility or capitulating to it, but by remaining secure even under attack, and by recognizing that the real opponent is not the other person or the other nation, but the conditioning that has convinced us we are enemies.

Eknath Easwaran p.121

When listening to people who are in conflict or when taking on a mediator role of listening to more than one side of a story, our own style of conflict resolution can influence our openness to what we hear. Again, we are asking ourselves to stay neutral and centered, putting our accustomed conflict style aside and listening to the deeper, unmet needs of others.

People have very different styles for dealing with conflict which are developed through personality, personal experience and cultural customs. This can be threatening to people who have a dissimilar style. It is helpful to be aware of the different ways people typically deal with conflict and to be aware of one's own style. One style is not better than another, just as one personality is not better than another — it's just different.

Thomas and Kilmann developed an often used Conflict Mode Instrument for determining styles of conflict behaviors. All modes are useful under certain conditions. However, without awareness and intention, people tend to resort to one mode which seems most familiar and therefore more comfortable, especially under stress.

Different styles are more appropriate for some situations and not for others. The collaborative style may serve as the ultimate ideal for the best interests of all parties in many situations, but it would not be appropriate in a volatile situation where immediate action is called for.

These modes are identified as:

- **Competing:** assertive, power-oriented, pursue own concerns; ideal is to bring out the best in us
- **Compromising:** finding an expedient, mutually acceptable solution which partially satisfies both parties; ideal is wanting both parties to come together, wanting resolution
- **Avoiding:** individual does not pursue his/her own concerns or those of the other; ideal is sidestepping the issue so as not to create problems and to maintain the relationship
- **Accommodating:** unassertive, the opposite of competing, individual neglects own concerns; ideal is selfless generosity, kindness and giving
- **Collaborating:** (win/win) empowerment of all people, assertive and cooperative, involving an attempt to work with the other person to find a solution which fully satisfies the concerns of both parties. It involves identifying underlying concerns and finding alternatives which meet both sets of concerns.

Collaborating between two parties might take the form of exploring a disagreement to learn from each other's insights, concluding to resolve some condition which would otherwise have them competing for resources, or confronting and trying to find a creative solution to an interpersonal problem.

(from Kenneth Thomas and Kilmann, Conflict Mode Instrument, XICOM,1979.)

Each one of us can identify with at least one familiar mode we may revert to under stress. Even when there are no apparent cultural differences, our past experiences with conflict have led us to take on one particular mode over others because it has worked in our favor.

Familiarity with styles helps us to see a behavior for what it is — a style — not necessarily a personal attack. It is really difficult to stay centered with an upset person who has an assertive, accusatory, style if one tends to avoid or accommodate in conflict. Conversely, an unassertive style is also difficult for someone who expresses feelings freely and attacks a problem.

It is clear that by compassionately listening to people in conflict, we are encouraging the collaborative mode. Many people are not familiar with this as a possibility for fear they will lose something in the process. Stating the collaborative mode as a goal is appropriate and steering the object of emotions away from people to the problem is a way of joining a person who may be exhibiting a "difficult" style. Ury and Fisher, in their book *Getting to Yes*, advise us to attack the problem, not the person. Deflecting the emotional intensity toward a problem and acknowledging another's pain and anger is healing and consistent with the principles of ultimate transformation of conflict. We are educators of the process as well as listeners.

SENSITIVITY TO CULTURAL DIFFERENCES

It is presumptive to believe our own approach is what is going to work in all situations. Cultural differences as well as individual styles can result in different behaviors and expectations. It is important to learn as much as possible about cultural customs of the people represented in the group in addition to familiarizing yourself with the issues, and the history of all sides.

When this is not possible, certain guidelines can be considered. An elicitive approach — that of asking people what they are comfortable with and what they would like you to know about their customs — is appropriate. What are the cultural precedents for situations like this? John Paul Lederach has compared elicitive and prescriptive approaches. Even when we know something works well, ie. Compassionate Listening, it does not serve to push it on others. Engaging people, asking for their input and inviting their participation, is the best way to teach anything. A truly elicitive approach is a very complex study because it is easy to assume so much. It is a fertile place for our blind spots to show up. It is an important subject to consider. Continual education and group discussion are helpful to unravel the intricacies of cultural expectations.

EMOTIONS

Many people have been marginalized and maligned by a dominant culture and are very angry. Their medium of expression might be difficult to listen to and the message can be lost in the delivery when we, as listeners, are attacked. It becomes even more important to remain compassionate and to see through the facade of anger to the underlying concerns and fears.

Acknowledging the attacker's feelings and validating their right to their perceptions is very powerful. Using reflective listening and understanding the feelings and frustrations will often engage them. People become more angry when they are expected to act as though they were calm. The bottom line is to listen, listen, listen without defense while being receptive to the feelings — yet not taking them on.

Leah Green writes of a highly emotional session in Israel. The names have been changed.

> *We were invited into the home of a resident of an Israeli settlement in the West Bank where we had an interview with Naomi, her husband Abraham and our friend, Rachel, whom we first met two years ago (Rachel had arranged this meeting for us in Naomi's home). The meeting ended on a painful note, when Naomi tapped into her tremendous anger and sadness about the loss of Jewish life in this conflict and began sobbing and lamenting.*

> *This was a very powerful meeting for many in our group. When Rachel walked us back to the bus stop down the street, I took the opportunity to talk with her. I said I heard her sorrow during the meeting about how it was no longer possible to be friends with the Palestinians as she and her family had been in the past. The last thing Rachel said to me as we kissed goodbye and I turned to board the bus was "Tamshichi Leah" meaning 'Continue the work!'*

There were mixed reactions from our group to the intense emotion released by Naomi. As she wailed for what seemed like a long time, unable to continue speaking, I sat there feeling sadness that our presence had brought up so much pain for her. I was also concerned that our tenuous contact with settlers would be broken by her discomfort. But when I heard Rachel's words to Leah, I realized that Naomi could have been grateful for the opportunity to express her emotions to a group of people who were willing to hear her pain. Both Naomi and Abraham had thanked us at the door for coming.

Sadness and pain are emotions which are difficult to experience and often make people uncomfortable. Too often, we want to jump in and, in some way, cut people off from their painful experience. A common way is to offer suggestions for solving the problem. Sometimes people worry that the emotions will never stop and that an intervention is needed. This is possible, yet quite unlikely. Sometimes, but most often not, it is appropriate to touch the person. The most contact I feel is appropriate is to move closer and to lean forward in the chair, and allow him/her the freedom and space to express. Embracing, even though that may feel like a natural response, often cuts people off from their feelings. They need most of all to know you are there. Holding the space is the greatest intervention you can make. It validates a person's strength and ability to cope.

**COMPASSIONATE LISTENING
LEVELS OF INVOLVEMENT**

CHAPTER 6

THE PRACTICE

The Compassionate Listening Project provides a roadmap for how to prepare oneself for involvement on any of many levels. Part of our mission is to provide education and to empower people to get involved and take leadership in the Compassionate Listening field.

There are many levels of involvement which we have identified. Since this work is always evolving, new ideas and projects will continue to unfold.

The Compassionate Listening Project provides guidance to individuals and groups;
  • to ensure people are adequately prepared and trained;
  • to maintain a high quality of Compassionate Listening training;
  • to share resources; and
  • to teach and learn from one another.

We encourage people to explore Compassionate Listening, and to discover where their unique gifts lie. Compassionate Listening starts within each of us as an internal process.

There are many levels of involvement in Compassionate Listening work. Here are some of the steps one can take to get involved:

  • Begin your personal practice with Compassionate Listening in your daily life;
  • Take a Compassionate Listening Introductory Workshop.
  • Start a Compassionate Listening study group in your community.
  • When your group feels ready, create a Compassionate Listening Project of your choice in your community.
  • Start a dialogue project in your community based on the principles of Compassionate Listening. This might be a Jewish-Arab group, a Jewish Group, an interfaith group; or a group which addresses any number of conflict issues.

  • If you are interested in teaching, first take a Training For Trainers Workshop with certified CLP trainers.
  • Co-facilitate with certified trainers for practicing group facilitation skills.
  • Consider taking mediation training in your community to build your facilitation/ negotiation/process skills.
  • Consider initiating a local or regional Compassionate Listening group where a committed study group would listen to leaders and community members in your area/region.

FEEDBACK

Each one of these steps involves a feedback loop which we feel is basic to building a strong and capable Compassionate Listening education system. In study groups, peers help each other by encouraging growth. When we start projects, it is important to get feedback from the group by asking for an evaluation of what they felt the benefits to be, and what suggestions they would make for the future. When facilitating for other trainers, they will offer feedback on strengths and needed areas of improvement. And trainers will ask for the same from facilitators and participants. The point is not to be critical, but to provide really helpful feedback and support. In this way, we can all be assured of a highly professional and compassionately personal program at every level of involvement.

STUDY GROUPS

Once you have started with the basic individual work, the next step is to join with others to form an informal study group in which you can practice the skills and get feedback. The essential components of a study group are those of creating a safe environment to work with others, and to enter that circle in a trusting way. Everyone needs people who are committed to the process of helping us see blind spots or shadow and to assist us in bringing awareness to them. Your study group will be an on-going classroom to hone and refine your skills. Everyone's life will be impacted by practicing in this way and it will provide tremendous learning for working with groups later.

What you practice in a study group will depend upon the interests and skills of your group. You can deepen the individual process already presented, select exercises from *Additional Exercises* in the *Appendix*, and develop processes of your own. Study groups also provide an opportunity to practice group facilitation skills.

PROJECTS

PLANNING

If you have prepared yourself through personal practice, have worked with others in a study group, and have completed a Compassionate Listening training, you are probably ready to embark upon a community or local, on-going project, or a delegation. Delegations consist of three or more people who visit a site for listening purposes.

When developing a project or forming a delegation, you are getting into group dynamics, which require facilitation skills in addition to a high degree of skill in Compassionate Listening. Projects force you to wrestle with the concepts and learn through "sitting in the fire."

The effectiveness of your project will be determined by careful planning.

Consult the chapter "Work in Action" for guidance. How you organize and what you do in the sessions will depend upon some of the following factors:

- intractability of the conflict
- number of participants
- number of meeting times possible
- experience of participants
- familiarity of participants with each other
- comfortable and friendly environment

BASIC GROUP FACILITATION SKILLS

Creating an environment where each person is respected and encouraged to participate is the first order of business. When we are facilitating people who are in conflict, bringing heart or compassion to the process creates a safe environment. It is a message to people they are not going to be attacked and therefore they do not need to be defensive. We are developing trust in order to express what is deeply troubling and needs healing.

The physical environment sets the scene for this sacred work. A quiet place where there are no interruptions honors the profundity of what transpires. We are creating a safe circle or container, so placing chairs in a circle is a way of reinforcing that image. As people contribute, they are making an offering to that sacred circle. A friendly and beautiful environment reinforces the qualities of safety and trust.

CREATING A SAFE CONTAINER

Convener(s) and leader(s), introduce yourself and tell people what brought you to the process: your background, credentials, and interest in the subject. People need to be assured they are in safe hands. You don't need to have a Ph.D. in the subject or years of training. If you behave authentically and have a sincere interest, people will respect your leadership.

People should be acknowledged and appreciated for coming, since it is assumed they did so voluntarily. Get assurances people came to work on the problem and want to create a better understanding and relationship. Dedicate what is accomplished to the greater good of all.

Pay attention to the diversity within and among members of a group. We want to avoid imposing our view and strive to let each group define and frame themselves. How do we communicate this openness as we teach? Find out what ethnic groups like to be called. Elicit from the group what ethnic, religious, social, diversities might surface and how they are to be handled.

Review a history of the issue and what led up to the meeting, acknowledging people who have been a part of the process. State the purpose and intent of bringing people together.

Identify roles and procedures.

The leader(s) are there to provide a safe place and process, and to facilitate communication.

The role of the participants is to be as open and honest with their thoughts and feelings as it is possible for them.

There needs to be intent to participate by communicating. Clarifying and understanding the problem is a first step. Resolving the problem may or may not be an expected outcome.

The group creates guidelines which will make the session work for them. Everyone needs to be part of this process and needs to fully agree with the guidelines. By so doing, they are giving permission to the leader to hold them to these guidelines. Write them on a large paper and place them on a wall visible to everyone in the room as a reminder.

Basic guidelines should include respect, confidentiality, timing. A list could consist of the following:
- Treat everyone with respect which means no interrupting, name calling, physical violence, or threats.
- Be inclusive.
- Express any dislikes to the whole group.
- Commit to stay with the process until complete.
- Be present and attentive.
- Respect confidentiality (This usually means no names are mentioned when discussing the events of the meeting with others; permission necessary to tape record; no quoting names in the media without permission; agreement to allow or not allow press coverage.)
- Time allowance for speaking (As a way of anticipating someone dominating, an agreed upon time from the group gives the group the responsibility rather than putting it on the leader. A time keeper can be chosen from the group.)

The group may come up with different suggestions. Asking them how they want to deal with strong emotions brings the issue to the forefront for discussion. Strong anger often leads to escalating emotions. When people are part of the agreement process, they are much more likely to stay within the set guidelines. Agreement and participation of the whole group is what matters. Open expression is harmless if not accusatory and blaming, sarcastic or mean-spirited. See *Additional Exercises* in the *Appendix* for working with anger.

INTRODUCTION OF PARTICIPANTS

Introductions serve as a way for people to enter this protected container which has been building to this point. They set the tone for the whole dialogue and offer a way for people to selectively share a piece of who they are with others. Everyone has an opportunity to enter the group and be seen and heard. Introductions are a way of including people in the process. People can remain in their chairs and introduce themselves. Sometimes it's a good strategy to get people to move about physically in an introduction. Allow people the same amount of time so no one person seems more important than anyone else.

WATCHING THE ENERGY

A major part of group facilitation requires an awareness of the energy field. Physical needs should be attended to by balancing long listening periods with a movement or a short break. Often people will not realize their own lack of energy or restlessness, so it requires the awareness of the leaders. If it's a large group, after the initial introductions to the whole group, there can be break-away groups with a facilitator. People can relay the essence of their small group discussions to the large group.

If people are showing distress by interrupting or showing strong emotions, the leader can call for a few moments of silence to hold the intention of the work. Silence can be called for by anyone in the group as a way of respecting something important that has just transpired, a point of emphasis, a way of acknowledging an intense emotion, or a plain "time-out." Silence can be as important as the conversation.

TEAM BUILDING

Team building exercises are used to reinforce a sense of community by solving a common problem or enjoying a common experience. They offer another way for people to build trust in each other and trust in the process. They can also provide an element of fun, which in and of itself, provides group bonding. Use these exercises with discretion as sometimes they are not needed and/or are not appropriate for your group.

TRAINING

At some point you may feel that you are ready to train others in Compassionate Listening through teaching workshops and classes. But we offer a word of caution: don't jump into teaching too quickly. We have been involved in our projects for at least five years and only now feel ready to teach and guide others. People wishing to become trainers must complete a *Training For Trainers Workshop* and demonstrate adequate standards for teaching this material.

FACILITATING FOR TRAINERS

The next stage of preparation is that of facilitating for trainers who are conducting basic and specialized training sessions. It is excellent experience to facilitate a master teacher and the training is greatly enhanced when there are experienced facilitators to work with small groups within the training. A facilitator becomes available for teaching, modeling, coaching and supporting small groups of people within the larger training context. Facilitating under the leadership of an experienced trainer is considered an internship and preparation for taking on the role of a trainer.

CONTINUING EDUCATION

Continuing growth and education is recommended throughout all these steps of involvement. If, however, one plans to become a trainer, we recommend you prepare your group facilitation skills. A background in conflict resolution is very helpful. Mediation and negotiation skills are also essential to working with groups in conflict and in training others. This level of the work requires a professionalism gleaned through education, personal growth and practice.

PART THREE:
THE WORK IN ACTION

*Never doubt that a small group of thoughtful, committed people
can change the world; indeed, it's the only thing that ever has.*

Margaret Mead

*What (our experiences) all share is a sense of humility
that comes when you feel a part of a world in which you are
of no lesser or greater importance than any other part.
And it is the allowance of that to continue that is important.*

Jeff Parker, Anchorage

THE WORK IN ACTION

Projects differ depending upon factors which include:

- Numbers of people involved
- Location and logistics
- Budgetary considerations
- Intensity of the conflict
- Time
- Purpose

An intended outcome of the Compassionate Listening projects described in this manuscript is to ultimately bring people together, face to face. In some cases, agreements are made. In other cases, listening to the concerns of others is the goal.

Bringing people face to face may have to be done in increments. Our project has brought people together in many different ways. Israeli residents have sometimes accompanied the American and Canadian delegates for interviews and homestays. Video has been used to show conflicted people the faces of their "enemy." We have also conducted residential Compassionate Listening training workshops for Israelis and Palestinians together. Bringing people with protracted conflict together is delicate and has to be carefully structured.

The Alaska Project is increasing exposure to the differing parties by relaying the concerns of one group to another, using quotes and filmed interviews. The groups have been separated by great distances. The next step will be to actually bring the groups face to face.

Gene Knudsen Hoffman uses a structured, deep dialogue as a first step which can bring conflicting parties together in small groups.

Rural Southern Voice for Peace (RSVP) conducts personal one-on-one listening interviews by going door to door asking people their views. This is often a first step toward developing a dialogue group which brings conflicting people together in groups. RSVP works internationally as well as in the United States

Dialogue groups within a community have more access to each other. They often meet for ongoing periods to deepen the conversation and contact over an issue. Sometimes mutual projects become part of the interaction as in the case of the Israeli/Palestinian Livingroom Dialogue Project.

Practice Groups meet to study and practice the skills. One has spawned a Listening Council which provides a healing environment where people are listened to non-judgmentally, thus providing a new approach to conflict resolution.

CHAPTER 7

THE COMPASSIONATE LISTENING PROJECT

Peace is not a prize won in negotiation.

Peace means seeing and hearing the humanity in the other.

Peace means starting not with assumptions about negotiations, but rather about wholeness in another human being.

Cantor Robert Scherr, MECD Delegate

I have to have hope. It's the only way I can live.

Hisham Sharabati, Palestinian Journalist

PROJECT SUMMARY
Written by Leah Green, Director

It's 1991. The first Intifadah is raging. A group of Americans walks quietly through the twisted alleys of al-Fawwar refugee camp near Hebron. We can hear Israeli soldiers moving through the other side of the camp. We turn a corner and come upon a middle-aged Palestinian woman picking through rubble. Our host explains to her that we have come to listen to the people of Israel and Palestine – to see the situation first-hand and listen to their stories.

As our host translates, we learn that until recently, the pile of rubble was her home. She cries with rage as she tells us that her youngest son was shot and killed by the Israeli army and her oldest son has just been sentenced to life in prison by a military court. After the sentence was handed down, her home was bulldozed. She and her two daughters are left with only the make-shift shed that housed their animals. The woman begins to wail: "Why do you Americans hate us? What have we done to you? We've lost everything! We are just struggling to survive..." We stand in shock as she continues to give voice to her anger and her grief.

Then, quite unexpectedly, she takes out a handkerchief, wipes her eyes, and invites us inside her shed for tea. We sit with her on her

dirt floor, drinking watered down, sweet tea, and begin to listen to one another. This was the participants' first awareness that many Palestinians believed the United States was waging war on them.

The Compassionate Listening Project, founded in 1996, evolved from these early citizen delegations. We are a non-profit organization dedicated to fostering conflict transformation and reconciliation through the cultivation and practice of deep listening skills.

We offer:
- Compassionate Listening workshops with a track for trainers' certification;
- Citizen delegations to the Middle East; and
- Educational outreach such as video production.

MID-EAST CITIZEN DIPLOMACY
Our work has developed over many years of practice in Israel and Palestine with our Mid-East Citizen Diplomacy project. We have been leading citizen delegation to Israel, the West Bank and Gaza since 1990.

Our delegations generally begin in Jerusalem with an intensive training in Compassionate Listening. We then practice our skills with a wide spectrum of Israelis and Palestinians, including religious and political leaders, ordinary citizens, peace activists and extremists.

There are many courageous Israelis and Palestinians who have much to teach us and who benefit from on-going support from the international community. Part of our time is spent learning from and supporting those already involved in reconciliation efforts.

We also hold Compassionate Listening workshops for Israelis and Palestinians and invite them to come together to practice with one another.

Leading Israeli and Palestinian professionals in the conflict resolution field serve on our Advisory Board and are actively involved with our delegations. Through our daily practice in the field and our group sessions, participants come away with a thorough understanding of Compassionate Listening as a tool for reconciliation.

Our delegations create a climate conducive for peace building. Participants come from a wide range of backgrounds; our last few delegations have included both Arab and Jewish-Americans. Participants come away transformed by the process and the people we interview express gratitude for an opportunity to really be heard. We have a skilled Compassionate Listening trainer/group facilitator on each trip. Participants meet frequently to reflect on and process their experience. This helps ensure a productive group process in a very challenging and stressful environment.

We support participants after their return home with guidance for sharing their experience in their communities. We connect them to our advisory board members and our larger participant group for support and networking. We also offer a trainers' certification track for those who would like to teach Compassionate Listening.

Many of our alumni are very active in their communities and present their experiences with The Compassionate Listening Project in a variety of community forums, inviting audiences to get involved in various ways. Some of our participants have joined or founded Jewish-Palestinian dialogue groups upon their return home.

We produced a beautiful, thirty-minute video, *Children of Abraham*, filmed during an all-Jewish Compassionate Listening delegation. Participants often use the video in their community presentations after their experience with the Project. It introduces the Compassionate Listening model and is a wonderful tool for dialogue as it humanizes a broad spectrum of Israelis and Palestinians. It also screens at religious institutions, universities, conferences and film festivals around the world. We also produced a companion video with Israelis and Palestinians – again from a wide spectrum - speaking in greater depth about the conflict. The new video is over an hour in length, and was filmed during delegations in 2001 and 2002. (Both are available from The Compassionate Listening Project and can be ordered directly from our website.)

Our model, to date, has been to arrange interviews with people from all sides of the conflict. After 12 years and 18 delegations, we have close connections within many sectors of society in each community. Several of our Israeli and Palestinian colleagues serve as ground coordinators and help us with scheduling. Some of our encounters are spontaneous, for example, during our homestays with families, rich opportunities for listening take place with various family members, neighbors and community leaders. We join people in their homes, offices, community centers, and in our hotel. We introduce our Project (well-known to many by now), state our purpose and ask to hear how the conflict affects them personally and how they envision their future. If a speaker has difficulty talking on a personal basis, we will often interject an open-ended question that directs attention to a more personal account. It is a sensitive process.

Many people in Israel and Palestine have experienced great personal suffering and it is difficult in many cases for the speaker to talk about these events with a group of strangers. Talking about their suffering can also retraumatize the individual. The listeners' expectations must be realistic – listeners must be careful not to push beyond what's comfortable for the speaker. Just providing the space can be a deeply healing process for the speaker. (Cultural considerations are also important and have been discussed in *Chapter Five*.)

The Compassionate Listening Project is respected among Israelis and Palestinians because of our intention to listen instead of offering advice – a common complaint about international delegations. They also know that we meet with a wide spectrum of Israelis and Palestinians. People we listen to appreciate our commitment to understand all perspectives, which generates a good deal of trust. Sometimes this also affords us the opportunity to bring the human face of one side to another. For example, if our speakers see our itinerary, they may ask what we heard from an adversary. We have often ended up playing the role of mediator, and many times we are able to humanize the other side. Because it's not easy to bring Israelis together with Palestinians from the West Bank and Gaza, we are beginning to use video tapes to share interviews from one side with another.

We also offer Compassionate Listening workshops for Israelis and Palestinians. A very diverse group has asked us for training so they can continue the work and train people in their own communities. We are especially excited about the potential benefits to those already involved in dialogue and coexistence work. Often, groups come together and have difficulty getting past positions. As is true in most situations, people would rather talk than listen and a discussion can quickly digress into an argument and suffering competition.

Another important aspect of our work has been to bring people of all sides together for public events hosted by institutions in each community. We provide a safe umbrella for people form all sides of the spectrum to come together to talk and listen to one another.

In 2002 The Compassionate Listening Project expanded our citizen delegations to Syria and Lebanon. We also birthed a new project in Germany for German and Jewish participants (the Jewish participants travel to Germany for the 10-day project).

We invite you to visit our website to learn more about our work and check on our upcoming delegations and workshops. You'll find articles, our newsletter and photo galleries of our current work. You can also sample our traveling Photo-graphic Exhibition on Compassionate Listening, and order our videos.

We would be happy to present a Compassionate Listening workshop or seminar at your college, institution, congregation or community group.

Contact information:

The Compassionate Listening Project
P.O. Box 17
Indianola, WA 98342
Phone: (360) 297-2280
Email: office@mideastdiplomacy.org
www.mideastdiplomacy.org

Marion Pargaman, an Israeli social worker, founded Mifgash, a non-profit organization whose goal is to contribute to resolving conflicts and to building peace in Israeli society. She has also created a dialogue group for Palestinians and Israelis called "The Circle for Sanity" which is grounded in non violence and spirituality. Marion is a part of Thich Nhat Hanh's Sanga in Jerusalem.

PEACE IS AROUND THE CORNER
by Marion Pargaman

I would like to tell you about a quite extraordinary event that happened to me during the walk organized by Tovana, the Vipasana meditation group in Israel.

What happened was a very personal experience but I feel it is important to share it with other people. The walk took place on the first week of April. It intended to give an opportunity for Palestinians and Israelis to walk together, to develop dialogue and self introspection, inspired by the ancient traditions that guided people like Mahatma Gandi and Martin Luther King. What I experienced on the last day was very much in the spirit of peace and coexistence, of calm and serenity created by the walk in the midst of the atmosphere of insanity and violence around us.

During 8 days, participants walked together from Tel Aviv-Yaffo to Jerusalem, passing by Jewish and Arab towns and settlements, in silence and awareness, declaring a commitment to deep listening and non-violence.

I joined the Walk with a group of Palestinians and Israelis who practice meditation and mindfulness together according to the tradition of Thich Nhat Hanh, a Vietnamese Zen Buddhist monk and famous peace worker. I participated in several days of the Walk. Monday 8th of April, the last day of the Walk, was the eve of the Holocaust day, a day of deep emotion for the Jewish community. It went from Ein Kerem, through Jerusalem to the foot of the old city walls. I planned to join the group from the morning, but after a sleepless night I decided to join later.

In the early afternoon I park my car at the final meeting place of the walk. I walk up to the walls of the old city, to meet them on their way. When I get to Jaffa gate, I find myself in front of a very agitated elderly Arab man exchanging insults with an elderly religious Jew who is standing at a bus station a few meters lower down.

Some policemen from a Border Police patrol are trying to calm them down, so that it won't turn into a fight, as they are extremely angry.

I stand beside the Arab, I speak to him calmly and ask him to sit down without reacting to the other's provocation. I am quite impressed by the restraint shown by the policemen. They don't defend one side or the other and respect both sides.

The bus arrives, the Jewish man boards the bus and the situation seems to have settled down. Then, a Jewish woman who was there in the queue from the beginning of the argument, and who did not get into the bus, takes upon herself to start insulting the Arab who reacts immediately.

The police have gone and I am left alone to try to calm the situation. I give my attention to the Arab who would have stayed quiet if he was not continually provoked by the woman. I try from a distance to reason with her without success.

She stops a passing police car and says something to the policeman who walks up to the Arab. I explain to him what is going on and he goes back to the woman. I am so happy that all the policemen in this situation act so calmly and help to restore peace.

Then, a Palestinian woman on her way to Jaffa gate bursts onto the scene; she jumps to the conclusion that the old Arab is under "attack" and rushes in a frenzy to rescue him. She yells some insults at the Jewish woman who was beginning to calm down, and the situation heats up again. All my attention is now focused on her. I feel she is like a bomb ready to explode.

I try to explain to her what is going on, but she is furious with me, screaming out her hatred, her despair and her pain. This is Palestine accusing Israel. At this moment I represent Israel for her. This whole situation is greater than the two of us and takes on proportions beyond our present meeting.

She shouts out her sorrow about what is going on now in the territories, the military incursions into Palestinian towns. She talks in particular about Jenin where some terrible fighting is now taking place. She has family and friends there and she says that our soldiers are war criminals. She is convinced that we want to kill them all. Why do we hate them so much? They are not responsible for the Holocaust, why should they be paying the price?

She tells me about the refugees and their constant suffering for which we are responsible. Pointing at the Jewish woman, she assures me that this Sephardi woman was treated with honor, as a human being, in an Arab country from where she comes, and look at how she behaves with Palestinians now!

It goes on and on; she shouts and spews her hatred for Israel at me. I don't try to argue with her at all. I don't show any reaction to all these accusations. I feel a huge compassion and an intense need to listen to her, only listen to her. My patience is nourished by understanding that behind this overwhelming hatred is a deep suffering and pain aggravated by the present situation of war. It must express itself in some way so that healing can take place.

I am ready to listen to what appears to me as the worst accusations, distortions or calumnies, without reacting. I am aware that what reinforces my strength at this moment is that I have absolutely no doubt that the suffering and pain of the Israeli people is not less real and legitimate. I don't let myself get tempted or trapped into guilt or anger. I am sorry for the tragedy on both sides. My compassion for her is not on the account of the compassion and sense of loyalty I have for my own people, for myself.

For me this is not an issue of who is right and who is wrong. I feel very very calm and peaceful deep inside. I know that it is the only way to calm her fury. I let her express herself for a long time without interrupting her. As she continues to shout at me, I tell her that she has no need to speak so loudly because I am listening to her with all my attention. At the same time I find myself caressing her arm. She lets me do it and progressively lowers her voice, while continuing to let her despair overflow.

She says to me: "Do you understand why some of us come and commit suicide among you? You kill us anyway, so why not kill you at the same time?" She even mentions the possibility of coming and blowing herself up out of despair. I tell her softly that I don't want her to die. Nobody should come to this decision. We all suffer on both sides. She goes on and on claiming that the Zionists only want to get rid of the Palestinians. I tell her: "You see I am a Zionist and I don't want to get rid of you. I wish we could live together as good neighbors". She listens to me!

She tells me about the demonstration that took place the week before near Ramallah. She complains about the Jewish organisations who took part in it. Then she asks me to donate some money to buy phone cards for Palestinians who need them. I give her some money. At this stage

the conversation is quite normal between us. She doesn't shout any more; she is even able to listen to me.

She is almost calm when I notice the people of the Walk approaching us slowly, at the top of the street. They are in a line, a hundred of them, one after the other walking in silence, slowly, quietly, aware of each step, creating an atmosphere of peace and safety around them. They are very present. They radiate calm and warmth. I point them out to her and explain that this is the reason I came here, to join a walk of peace in which Palestinians and Israelis are together. I tell her about the Walk, its message of coexistence and peace; peace at every step, here and now.

I suggest that she come into the line with me. She hesitates and rejects my offer. At this moment they reach us. Several people I know shake my hand warmly as they go by. A young woman very active in a group of rapprochement between the two peoples, approaches her and gives her a kiss. It appears that they know each other. I notice that she is very moved by the Walk and the atmosphere it radiates. She seems to me calmer and calmer. Nothing like the furious woman I met only several minutes before.

The end of the line passes by us and I want to join it. Again I invite her and again she declines. I tell her that I understand and respect her decision. Before I go I tell her: "I am sure that some day we will succeed in building peace between us." She smiles and replies: "Me too".

Then to my total surprise, she comes close to me and kisses me on my cheeks! She walks alongside the line for a while. She tells me that she likes this Walk, that it makes her feel good, gives her relief and that her mood is much better now. I am very very moved. I feel overwhelmed by this encounter, especially by its unexpected ending. Peace was there around the corner, I did not miss it!! I was aware that an intense moment of real reconciliation had taken place. Everything contributed to it. Incredible timing that brought me to this place at this time; that brought her, in her turn, with enough time to first pour out her anger, to receive needed listening and compassion, time to calm down, so that she could be receptive to the subtle quiet energy of the Walk.

The Walk, emanating intense healing, bringing the tangible presence of peace and goodwill of a whole organised group, appeared just in time to complete the scene, adding a wider perspective to an individual encounter. The thick walls of her hatred were shattered allowing her to express what was deep in her heart. Kissing me was a miracle! Within a short period of time, laden with emotions, her energy of hatred and death underwent an incredible transformation.

I don't know if, or how quickly, she returned to her initial state or how long she remained calm. I know that this profound transformation was very real and intense; no matter what followed, it will leave a trace and a memory that cannot disappear. A seed of peace was sown in her heart. We must plant many more, and water them thoroughly. I never understood so fully the deep meaning of the words pronounced by Thich Nhat Hanh in Shanghai on 19th October, after the 11th September tragedy:

"Terror is in the human heart. We must remove this from the heart. Destroying the human heart, both physically and psychologically, is what we should avoid. The root of terrorism is misunderstanding, hatred and violence. This root cannot be located by the military. Bombs and missiles cannot reach it, let alone destroy it. Only with the practice of calming and looking deeply can our insight reveal and identify this root. Only with the practice of deep listening and compassion can it be transformed and removed. Darkness cannot be dissipated with more darkness. More darkness will only make darkness thicker. Only light can dissipate darkness. Those of us who have the light should display the light and offer it so that the world will not sink into total darkness."

This story is not mine alone. I know I have the duty to tell it to as many people as possible, so that planting seeds of peace may go on and on.

Marion Pargamin, Jerusalem

CHAPTER 8

HEALING OUR COMMUNITIES

Do you truly know what is positive and what is negative? Do you have the total picture?
There have been many people for whom limitation, failure, loss, illness, or pain in whatever form
turned out to be their greatest teacher. It taught them to let go of false self-images and
superficial ego-dictated goals and desires.
It gave them depth, humility, and compassion. It made them more real.

Eckhart Tolle

BACKGROUND

Entering this new millennium, I had been praying for more peace in the world. The celebrations held around the world heralding this new age gave me hope for healing our global community. And yet, here in the Seattle area, we were feeling the threat of terrorism, as our border patrol arrested someone entering our country with explosives.

With the threat of terrorism and at the same time, a number of my friends in partnership breaking up, I realized there was a great need for healing on all levels. I had been attempting to stay supportive of each person and found that I was lacking the skills to bring peace to their disputes. It became difficult to go to any community activity without their angry feelings showing up. Whom shall I invite for a community or holiday dinner, and whom shall I exclude because of their anger? I saw that the seeds of global conflict were present in my dearest friends. I saw that some kind of healing modality was wanted and needed that didn't yet exist. I felt inspired to create a community based council to support healing these conflicts.

I began to share my vision with some good friends about starting a *Listening Council*. Many were enthusiastic, feeling the great need in our community for a safe council of peers. So I

further investigated what skills we would need to bring to this new work. Having Leah Green in my community helped a great deal, for I knew of her work and asked for her support which she generously gave. Wanting to have leadership of both genders, I invited a close woman friend, Therese Charvet, who had years of leadership experience in women's groups, to co-facilitate this work with me.

THE WEEKLY PRACTICE GROUP

We drafted a letter (November 2001), citing the ruptures in our community and the tragedy of 9/11 as good reasons to come together for some healing. We invited friends to come learn the helpful skills of Compassionate Listening and begin to heal our own conflicts as a path toward making the world a safer place to live. I then took the Compassionate Listening training and invited those in the training to also partake in this group. From this weekly practice group, I envisioned that we would hone our skills and hold special *Listening Councils* for when it would be needed by community members.

We started with twenty participants and currently average 14 at each weekly meeting. The participants range in age from 18 to 64 and there is usually an equal number of men and women. The group welcomes all those who are interested in learning and practicing Compassionate Listening. The group primarily consists of "regulars" who participate weekly with newcomers showing up once or twice a month.

OVERVIEW OF EACH MEETING

- Meditation to clear our minds and become more present in the moment.

- A non-verbal exercise designed to help everyone feel more connected to the others in the group.

- A verbal check-in from each person without cross talk. This begins our practice of listening to each other with our hearts.

- A monthly teaching exercise to advance our skill in Compassionate Listening.

- Each participant indicates whether they want to be a speaker or listener; we break into large or small groups to do our Compassionate Listening practice.

- To close we gather together as one group, and wrap up by doing some debriefing about what was experienced and learned in the practice sessions.

OUR TIPS SHEET FOR COMPASSIONATE LISTENING "PRACTICE"

- Stay Present
- Don't try to "Fix It"
- Watch your Judgements
- Allow Silence
- Don't ask "Why?"
- Avoid "yes" and "no" type questions
- Listen with your heart and not your head

LISTENING COUNCIL: A CIRCLE FOR CONFLICT RESOLUTION, PERSONAL GROWTH AND COMMUNITY HEALING

VISION

We envision a world where communities provide love, support and compassionate listening to those in conflict and/or personal crisis. We envision a community where everyone feels like an "insider" and everyone's gifts are seen, valued and contribute to the wholeness and health of the community.

WHAT WE DO

When called by someone in conflict or in personal crisis, we create a circle of peers who gather in Council to listen, and create an opportunity for that person to be seen, acknowledged and heard. When the situation involves a conflict with others who are interested in Listening Council as a tool for resolution, we meet with all involved parties separately and then together. The Councils provide a forum for the resolution of conflicts, both inner and outer. Listening Councils offer a safe place to express emotion, an opportunity for the depth of the difficulty to be revealed and accepted, and a way through the suffering into a new freedom where the gifts of the situation can be identified and appreciated.

HOW IT LOOKS

Councils consist of anywhere from 2-10 people, including at least one person trained in Compassionate Listening techniques who acts as facilitator. Sometimes specific listeners are specially invited by the person requesting the Council; other times the call for listeners goes out to our practice group and the Council consists of whoever can show up at the designated time. Peer listeners are motivated because of their personal connection to those in crisis and their desire to give back the support and love they have received during their own challenges and conflicts. Councils may meet only once, or in the case of conflicts with others, several times. Each Council generally lasts 1 to 2 hours.

INTENTION

- To create a new approach to conflict resolution
- To create a healing environment, a safe space where transformation can occur
- To listen fully, with a quiet mind without judgement
- To offer love and support rather than advice and problem-solving

- To help each person discover his/her own inner wisdom
- To dig deeply into what is underneath conflicts and challenges
- To identify and release blame and judgement toward oneself and others
- To see what there is to learn in challenges and conflicts, to "find the pearl"
- To help identify and articulate unmet needs
- To catalyze growth, spiritual and emotional evolution
- To heal the isolation of modern communities
- To offer perspective

VALUES

Listening Council is not aligned with any particular religion or brand of spirituality; it is not therapy. It is built on the following universal truths:
- Full hearted listening generates healing, transformative energy
- Challenges and conflicts provide an opportunity for self-discovery
- The outer life is a reflection of the inner life
- A common cause of suffering is personal thought patterns that hold us as "victim"
- Humility, acknowledging how much we do not know, is a key to conflict resolution
- Personal freedom comes from forgiveness and reconciliation
- The heart, not the head, is the place for healing to happen
- Mindfulness is an essential pathway to healing
- Nonjudgemental peer listening models how to be compassionate with ourselves
- Acceptance of "What is" is the key to healing
- We are all both students and teachers in the lessons of life

CHALLENGES

- Bringing more facilitation into each session: we recognize that without good facilitators the person who is speaking can remain stuck in their story. We are developing a preparatory information sheet, which will help prepare the speaker for their *Listening Council.* We are gathering feedback from each Council to help improve our skills.

- Listeners have varying degrees of Compassionate Listening skills, so we have been occasionally sidetracked by questions or advice-giving that have not helped the speaker. We are developing ways to cultivate better listening such as including a mindfulness bell that the facilitator will ring when some one gets off track or there is need for silence. We are refining our understandings and awareness in our written "Tips for our listeners."

- We recognize that *Listening Council* is not therapy and that those in conflict may need professional help in addition. On the other hand, we see the healing value of peers supporting those who they care about within the context of community. We have seen some amazing results from this model.

- The amount of time it takes to bring each relationship conflict into a state of reconciliation. When people are in conflict, it requires meeting with each person individually at least once, until such time as we sense they are ready to walk in the shoes of the other(s), and then to meet with them together once or twice. On the other hand, we experienced a sense of great success with a woman who had been marginalized by the community because of her anger, judgements and blame and needed 5 Councils to work through it all. In the end she came to a place of love and acceptance and reconnection in community. This kind of success rewards all our time and effort.

NEXT STEPS

In the future, when our skills are strong and the time feels right, we will offer *Listening Council* to a broader community and will request financial compensation for our time and effort. We envision that we will provide skilled leadership and facilitation, requesting volunteer listeners to join us in *Listening Council* from among the person-in-need's network of friends and family. This will serve the dual function of providing the service as well as spreading the skills and benefits of "Compassionate Listening" to a broader audience.

We are working on a workshop/training so we can share this model and create a network of *Listening Councils*.

Contact Information:
Brian Berman
PO Box 975
Suquamish, WA 98392
360/779-1223
rockcarver@earthlink.net

Therese Charvet
9333 Holly Farm Ln.
Bainbridge Island, WA 98110
206/842-7141
therese@bainbridge.net

STORY FROM MONDAY NIGHT GROUP

This is a story of how listening can begin a healing process that shifts the way an individual responds to life. It is the story of how one of our Community Practice Group participants took responsibility for her needs.

Jan has been coming to our Compassion-ate Listening Practice group since it first began. She is bright and very quick to respond in anger when not feeling safe or heard. She had no previous experience with Compassionate Listening but was studying Marshall Rosenberg's Non-violent Communication, and was earnestly growing this new side of herself. She came to practice weekly with an enthusiasm for learning Compassionate Listening skills. One session went something like this:

Jan settled into her seat at one end of the room where everyone was able to see her. She began to tell us how she had just taken a leap of faith and resigned from her job. She said that she felt as though she had jumped off a cliff and was suspended in the air without anything supporting her. She spoke about her cartoon character totem, the coyote in the Road Runner cartoon, who keeps getting himself blown up. As she deepened into her story of an

abusive childhood and no modeling of how to develop her skills, she said that she learned how to fake her way into new areas of interest. She cited how, in her adult life, she found jobs by being confi-dent, asking for manuals on computers and just being a fast learner.

She said she felt like a fake, and was soon to explode like her cartoon character. She began to get very emotional, talking about her home and the mess that it was in. She began to tell story after story of how she had been a failure at the most basic of home ownership and home care, that her power had been cut because she had not paid the bills and how metaphoric that was. She was clearly in pain and she sobbed deeply.

The group had been listening and in the silence there was that pregnant time where someone was going to speak. The first compassionate listener, a newcomer to the group, began by asking Jan if he might share how he had dealt with a similar.....and before he could even finish what he wanted to say, Jan said, "I wish you wouldn't." Then another listener asked "Why"? Jan quickly retorted, "Number 5 on the chart says 'Don't ask 'why' questions.' Jan was training us, though this was her curt way of responding to protect her wounds. She then paused and in the quiet she asked, "Can I just have some empathy?"

The group softened, our hearts are going out to her in a loving way. This was reflected back to her. We weren't quite sure what was beneath the statement and we wanted to learn more. There were a few acknowledging statements made to her. Jan sobbed some more and then said that she had never had a community before or a group that accepted her so fully. She said that by our accepting her without judgement and love, she was beginning to be able to accept herself.

C H A P T E R   9

THE DAUGHTERS SISTERS PROJECT

"I look forward to Tuesday all week long. Being in group is the most
important thing I do. There's nowhere else where I can be totally myself and
know that I won't be rejected for who I am and what I feel or what I've done.
In group I can hear myself think. Even when I ran away from home that time,
and quit school, I never stopped going to group. If that doesn't say
everything, then shit, I don't what does? "

Erin, Girls Focus Group member

PROJECT SUMMARY
Written by Linda Wolf

The Daughters Sisters Project:
Girls Talking Circles - Young Women
Speaking and Listening from the Heart

In the spring of 1993, therapist, Wind Hughes and I invited a diverse group of young women ages 14-21 to meet with us once a week to help us with a book we were writing for teen girls. We called our group the Girls Focus Group (talking circle) and planned to meet for 10 weeks. Our intention was to talk about the issues we knew middle and high school girls were facing, issues we had been through ourselves as young women and in many ways were still dealing with as adults. Things like self-love, body image, sexuality, peer pressure, relationships, substance use, stereotypes, emotions, and insecurity.

While our goal was to gather research for the book, it quickly became clear that the talking circle itself was critical for these young women and they begged us not to stop. For many of them, it provided the *only* safe space they had where, as one of our advisors, Carol Gilligan, said, "they could say what they think, hear, feel and see." The group grew organically as we incorporated new paradigms in feminist/woman-

ish thinking, and practiced trust building and conflict resolution processes that we'd learned from such mentors as Marshal Rosenberg, Arnie Mindell, Danaan Parry, Riane Eisler, Marion Woodman and Bell Hooks, pioneers in the fields of conflict resolution, cultural transformation, psychology, communication, systems theory, and inner healing.

Talking and listening to each other gave the girls a rare chance to hear their own and others' voices, see that they were not alone, and understand that they need not be destroyed by their issues but could become empowered to change them. The group ended up staying together for 2 years, during which time we also created a young men's talking circle, as well as a mixed gender circle, called GenderTalks. The book, *Daughters of the Moon, Sisters of the Sun: Young Women and Mentors on the Transition to Womanhood* was based on the lives of these young people, and released in 1997. It has sold over 20,000 copies, and is currently being translated into Chinese.

Since then, we've received hundreds of requests from young people and adults asking how they can start talking circles in their communities. To meet this request, we developed *the Art of Facilitating Teen Talking Circles* workshops, and over the past six years our teens and adults have trained over 500 facilitators from the US and

Canada to start circles or use our model in their existing work.

One of the most important additions to our work has been to become involved with the Compassionate Listening Project and bring the skills we've learned in their workshops into ours. In many ways, compassionate listening, as taught by the Compassionate Listening Project, was the missing piece in our work. While we had already been practicing deep listening, we now have a much stronger ability to impart the skills necessary for young people to replicate what they do in circle outside in daily life with their friends, families, teachers and others.

This year, the Auburn AmeriCorps Team was the first in Washington State to ask us to provide their staff with an Introduction to Compassionate Listening Workshop. And due to the results of this workshop have now requested a full Compassionate Listening Training to be incorporated into the Art of Facilitation workshops we provide them. As Bill Mandeville, Director of the Auburn Neighborhood Project said, "Clearly, learning to listen compassionately and speaking from the heart go hand in hand in supporting our efforts to heal people one person at a time, and spread this healing to the students we work with, in our community, and throughout the world."

We are grateful to be part of the Compassionate Listening Project's certification process and look forward to being able to help more and more communities in their desire to help young women and young men be empowered and healthy through Girls Compassionate Listening Circles and GenderTalks.

Linda Wolf is the director of the Daughters Sisters Project and Global Youth Allies, and the co-author of two books including *Global Uprising: Confronting the Tyrannies of the 21st Century – Stories from a New Generation of Activists*, New Society Publishers, 2001 (www.globaluprising.net)

The Daughters Sister Project (www.daughters-sisters.org) is dedicated to educating, inspiring, and empowering young women, fostering part-nership and understanding between the genders, generations and cultures and supporting youth in positive self expression and social action for a just and sustainable world.

For more information, contact:
The Daughters Sisters Project
PO Box 4492
Rolling Bay WA. 98061

206-842-3000
daughtersi@aol.com

www.daughters-sisters.org
www.youthactivism.org
www.globaluprising.net

CHAPTER 10

ALASKANS LISTENING TO ALASKANS ABOUT SUBSISTENCE

I never did see urban people talk about their growing-up years -
and it's similar to ours....
You know, growing up in the village we get exposed
to the idea that automatically whiteman is trying to change our ways,
but there are some that live like we do.

Glenna Parrish, Buckland

Yes, we are going to find that there are differences that we can't reconcile,
and probably we don't need to. What we do need to do is respect the others' values.
If people are going to try to get together in spite of the differences, we are going
to have to learn to respect the differences and live with them.

Dick Bishop, Fairbanks

PROJECT SUMMARY

(Excerpted from *Alaskans Listening to Alaskans About Subsistence Update*, June 2000).

Alaskans Listening to Alaskans about Subsistence was started by Alaska Quakers and is being carried out by the American Friends Service Committee (AFSC), Alaska Quakers, and other groups and individuals committed to peace in the Alaskan community.

The project is structured as a series of small gatherings, visits and interviews in urban and rural communities. There is one paid staff person, and there are numerous volunteers around the State. Core funding comes from the American Friends Service Committee, with about 1/3 of the budget to raise from other organizations and individual donors.

We have been listening to other Alaskans — those with a direct stake in the subsistence debate — to understand the essential concerns of all involved. We now have a digital video camera, along with a computer with digital editing capability, which allows us to film the sessions with the goal of sharing the footage with both urban and rural participants. We've video-taped all sessions, and with the permission of the speakers, have begun to introduce different "sides" of the issue to one another.

There are probably as many "sides" to the question of subsistence as there are people concerned with it, but the debate is chiefly between those who support the rural preference as defined by Federal Law, and those who do not. While there are many Alaska Native people who live in urban areas, and over half of the population of the bush is non-Native, the debate is widely understood on cultural terms. So our first efforts have been to hear from those urban dwellers who seek equal access to resources, and from rural native people who see the Federal law as their best protection. We hope to expand these circles.

We are asking about experiences, values, concerns, hopes and fears. We are not looking for a particular outcome, but are working to build understanding and peace.

In the subsistence debate, urban-based hunters are afraid of losing an activity which is extremely important to them on many levels, and which often has been passed down from generation to generation. And like their rural counterparts, they are distressed by the split between Alaskans.

From rural residents, we've heard that theirs is a way of life under siege. Native villages are afraid of losing everything.

We have heard that Alaska Native people were told at statehood, and again when claims went through, that subsistence hunting and fishing rights would be protected. Instead, they have seen the State go back on its word, in declaring the rural preference "unconstitutional."

Villagers are frustrated with regulations made by outsiders which often do not match up with the reality of the subsistence hunting and fishing cycles. Speakers have expressed a strong interest in cooperative management schemes, and hope that joint management will come to pass. And despite frustration, people are willing to talk again in hopes of building bridges across the cultures.

For everyone from whom we have heard, the possibility of coming together across the divide comes down to respect. They tell us that mutual respect founded on real understanding of one another is the key.

Contact Information:
Cynthia Monroe, Director
Alaskans Listening to Alaskans About Subsistence
American Friends Service Committee
P. O. Box 110932
Anchorage, AK 99511
(907)278-2582
altas@alaska.net

CHAPTER 11

THE MAKAH WHALING COMPASSIONATE LISTENING

PROJECT SUMMARY

Written by Jeff Smith

HOW THE PROJECT STARTED

The Makah Indian Nation is a small tribe on the tip of the Olympic Peninsula in Washington State. In recent years it has received the support of the International Whaling Commission and the US Federal government to resume hunting the Pacific Gray Whale because of their remarkable recovery from the edge of extinction to return to historical numbers. Their resumption of whaling as a treaty right has led to protests from anti-whaling and animal rights groups fearful that this sets a precedent that will make it easier for others to resume whaling. Anti-Indian groups and bigoted individuals have piggy-backed on this highly visible and controversial issue to help stir up latent and create new negative feelings toward American Indians. Some of these individuals and groups have adopted such controversial actions as using boats to intercept the traditional whaling canoe. The US Coast Guard has rammed some of these anti-whaling water craft who have come within a specified safety zone around the whalers. There have been threats of violence, (including death threats) and bigoted messages sent through e-mail and left on answering machines of the Makah and supporting tribes as well as bomb threats directed at tribal schools.

Concerned individuals and representatives of human rights and ethnic organizations first met on July 7, 1999, forming the July Seventh Coalition. They set as their mission to work to bring more peace and understanding of the whaling issue while not taking a position for/or against whaling. The coalition decided that a Compassionate Listening project would be a powerful way to accomplish this, so a Reconciliation Committee of interested volunteers came together to carry out these activities. Compassionate Listening sessions with a trained group of listeners were held separately. The concerns of, first, the anti-whalers from protesting groups, and then the pro-whaling speakers from the Makah and other Indian tribes and their allies, would begin the process of indirect and then face-to-face dialogue between the groups. Other listening projects had shown how speaking and being heard would reduce frustration, and becoming acquainted at a personal and heart-felt level could increase interest and empathy in the other side while specific information could lead to greater understanding and compromises in attitudes and actions. It was not expected that positions on the issue would necessarily change.

HOW THE PROJECT HAS DEVELOPED IN THE LAST YEAR AND A HALF

This Reconciliation Committee spent some months studying the basic philosophy and ways to organize projects in Compassionate Listening. The following is a list of activities that have taken place since that time:

* Site visit to Neah Bay by members of the coalition to become acquainted with the Makah tribe's views and those of the Whaling Commission (October 30-31, 1999).

* Two-day Compassionate Listening training session for prospective listeners and the Recon-

ciliation Committee so they would be prepared for the non-adversarial, non-judgmental, objective listening the project requires (December 16,17 1999).

* The first formal listening session, held in Seattle, with six anti-whaling speakers and nine trained listeners (February 28, 2000).

* The second formal session with four supporters of whaling, two Makah anthropologist allies and a cultural leader from a supporting tribe (April 3, 2000).

* Two series of individual conversations with a few tribal members, some who supported whaling and one who did not, with a few of our trained listeners (May and June, 2000).

* Two series of listening sessions in the field with whaling opponents who were staying near the reservation during whaling season and pro-whalers on the reservation (May and June, 2000).

* Direct face-to-face weekend get-to-together with two pro-whaling Makah and a two whaling opponents in Neah Bay on the reservation, beginning with socializing over a salmon dinner on the beach and concluding with a deep discussion about feelings on whaling (July 15 and 16).

* Five Compassionate Listening training sessions that have included newcomers, recruits from the ranks of speakers from the formal listening project held earlier, attendees of the Quaker North Pacific Yearly Meeting and members the Port Angeles community near Neah Bay. The latter is starting another compassionate listening project to build bridges with another local tribe, the Lower Elwha S'Klallam.
Most of the listening sessions were video taped. Only two people actually declined, when asked, to be taped.

HOW THE RECONCILIATION COMMITTEE HAS CARRIED OUT ITS WORK

The committee prepared for some months by studying writings on Compassionate Listening, especially Gene Knudson-Hoffman's works. After learning more about the philosophy and skills

required, members of the July Seventh Coalition and friends visited Neah Bay to better understand the Makah perspective on the issues and conflicts. In December, a Compassionate Listening training session was organized for prospective listeners so they could better fulfill their roles as accepting listeners of the speakers viewpoints in a nonjudgmental, non-adversarial way. The project occurred in three phases:

1. Separate formal and informal listening sessions. A few speakers, first from one side and then the other, spoke in different sessions but to the same trained listeners.

2. Opportunities afforded for the committee to share some of the views of each side with the other.

3. Facilitated face-to-face meetings were held, so that participants could get to know each other and their concerns and continue the reconciliation process.

An additional bonus has been the participation of one pro-whaler and two anti-whalers in the Compassionate Listening training, so that they can become more involved in the project.

4. Another listening session in Neah Bay with one of the churches. This location was chosen because the people who were drawn to participating in either this project or the Compassionate Listening training came out of a spiritual/religious background.

HOW THIS PROCESS HAS FACILITATED RECONCILIATION

The resumption of Makah whaling has initiated a conflict. Each side feels their positions and perspectives are misunderstood and unheard. Tribal members believe their treaty rights are threatened, as well as their physical well-being. The anti-whalers fear they will fail in protecting the whales if the Makah whale hunt proceeds, and that this will lead to more widespread whaling around the word. Many of the anti-whalers feel that they are open-minded people, who however, absolutely draw the line at hunting and killing these Pacific gray whales. Some who are familiar with the anti-abortion/right-to-life movement compare the strong feelings about whaling to that issue. A whale's life is seen as important, or even more so, than a human's life.

Most feel that the tribal council runs the reservation like a dictatorship, that other tribal members are either the silent victims or are being duped, and that there is money in it for someone, which is the primary reason that whaling has been revived. An often stated alternative theory is that the Federal government is using the Makah whaling in some grander international game. In a session with both pro- and anti-whalers, there was some exploration of this idea, with common concern expressed. There is the sense that if the Makah people had the chance to see how much more they could gain by doing something other than killing the whales, they would do so. One speaker said that if the Makah insisted on maintaining its nationhood/tribal sovereignty, that the reservation's roads, power, cable TV, tourism and funding should be cut off. A general theme seems to be that the anti-whalers know what is really happening on the reservation better than the Makahs themselves do.

Although there has, at times, been a strong alliance among the anti-whalers to stop the whalers, it is clear that some of the individuals are against — or at least uncomfortable with — the statements or tactics of some of the other anti-whalers. The listeners have noted that at times the statements by some of the anti-whalers felt racist, bigoted, and self-centered, and that maybe some of the other speakers present at that session may have felt the same way. Two of these individuals have become involved in trying to find ways to engage more peacefully on this issue, even while they work to stop the whaling.

All of the Makah we have spoken to have put supporting their treaty above whatever personal position they have on whaling. In other words, they have decided to support it because it is what the tribe as whole has decided to do. Those who are personally against whaling, (and some are for) feel it actually diminished their treaty rights and tribal sovereignty to ask for the support of the US government in seeking the approval of the International Whaling Commission. There is a great deal of pride in the whaling heritage, and in the harvesting of the whale on May 17, 1999. Makahs who are most strongly

behind whaling most often cite cultural, spiritual and subsistence. Some Makah disagree as to whether these are valid reasons to hunt. They question if the methods used are traditional enough or if the whalers are pure enough spiritually, or if whale meat is important or essential to the Makah's diet.

The opportunity to speak in a heart-felt way in a safe setting can reduce the frustration and enable everyone to clarify their views in a more positive, less defensive way. Thus, it provides another model of conflict resolution in these community-wide issues. People can have dialogue with opponents which increases their understanding of opposing views by providing more information on the issues. New information and personal relationships can lead to appreciation and more empathy for alternative views. It can change attitudes and lead to reconciliation and peace rather than escalate defensiveness and hostility. As the number of moderate individuals increase during this process, the extremists will become more isolated and have less influence in their community.

Using Compassionate Listening to build bridges between American Indians and non-Indians shows great promise. Our speakers and trainees have almost unanimously endorsed it as showing great potential in this area. Virtually all tribes have various kinds of difficulties with their neighboring communities and Compassionate Listening could be a useful tool in ameliorating them. We see this project, as well as the Port Angeles/Lower Elwha Tribe Compassionate Listening project, as pilot projects to enhance relationships between these communities.

ADDENDUM

In our state, a recent controversy over differences in hunting regulations between Indian and non-Indian hunters was escalating toward hostility and violence. At the request of the tribal members, they called a meeting between some moderates from each group, with state representatives in attendance to answer questions. One decisive factor in the success of this effort was the greater knowledge gained by the non-tribal hunters about the importance to the tribes of their cultural and religious traditions as they related to hunting practices. As these groups began working out their differences and offered compromises, the non-Indian extremists had less support and influence in their community, and acts and threats of violence disappeared.

Contact Information:
Jeff Smith
American Friends Service Committee
814 NE 40th St.
Seattle, WA 98105
Phone: (206)632-0500 FAX: 632-0500
e-mail jsmith@afsc.org
www:july7coalition.org

C H A P T E R   1 2

RURAL SOUTHERN VOICES FOR PEACE (RSVP)

Every human being is an unfolding miracle,
yet along the path we all have experiences that leave us feeling angry, confused, fearful or disempowered.
These are the seeds of hatred, injustice and conflict. Deep listening doesn't side-step those experiences.
It meets them with empathy and compassion so that the people involved can begin to release their fears and go deep
into their center — into the essence of their humanity, where we find our real potential for justice and love.

Herb Walters, RSVP Founder

"I find Listening Projects to be a central ingredient in community development.
Communities have breached barriers, created partnerships, built capacity,
and moved forward with direct input and enthusiasm from residents."

Tom Fischer, Tallahassee, Florida

"The Listening Project has been essential to our civilian peace team work
in communities bitterly divided by ethnic fears and hatred. And our facilitated dialogue
between Catholic Croatians and Orthodox Serbs was very effective in enabling former enemies
to touch each others hearts."

Lidija Obad, Republic of Croatia

LISTENING AND DIALOGUE PROJECTS

(excerpted from materials published by RSVP).

The Listening Project, founded in 1981 by Herb Walters is an organizing tool for nonviolent social change, especially useful in communities where conflict or disempowerment weakens efforts toward community development, justice, peace, or protecting the environment. Listening Projects use trained volunteers to conduct one-on-one interviews that address local and some-times national or international issues. Interview-ers use deep listening and take time to build trust and understanding so that people inter-viewed can go deeper into their fears, hurts, hopes, needs, feelings and ideas. This heart-centered process helps reduce misinformation and stereotypes, opens new channels of commu-nication and education and helps develop "community based" strategies and programs for change. As citizens begin to understand that their feelings, opinions and actions can matter, they respond in dynamic ways. Some offer creative ideas and solutions. Some take the next step to action or leadership. The Listening Project then continues as a comprehensive community organizing process that utilizes citizen input, and leadership. Information from the listening interviews becomes the foundation for citizen empowerment, community improvement and social change. Thus Listening Projects follow much planning and training and may take six months to a year to complete.

RSVP PROJECTS

In **Harlan County, Kentucky,** a Listening Project helped empower citizens and strengthen the Concerned Citizens Against Toxic Waste (CCATW) in their campaign against toxic waste that was poisoning their water supplies. In **Baton Rouge, Louisiana,** The Racial Issues Listening Project helped civil rights activists find unexpected support in a community that had voted for a Nazi and Klansman. In **North Carolina,** a Listening and Dialogue Project broke through walls of hatred, fear and silence with a Listening Project and Facilitated Dialogue on religious intolerance towards homosexuals. In **St. Marys, Georgia**, peace activists seen as "outside agitators" demonstrating against nuclear weapons, were able to build common ground and find support with community residents including military base employees. In **Keysville, Georgia,** a Listening Project helped African-American organizers reduce racial conflict and citizen apathy that was hurting campaigns for clean water, literacy, and health services.

> *"I don't think we could have done this without Listening Project help. I believe they played a positive role in opening communication and helping us understand each other and how to work together."*
>
> Keysville Mayor Emma Gresham,
> in the Atlanta *Constitution*

RSVP has also trained listeners in Asia, Europe, Central America and other conflict areas around the world.

In August 1992, a Listening Project helped reduce ethnic tensions between Serbs and Muslims in the Serbian village of **Brestovac, Yugoslavia.** In the **East Slavonia region of Croatia,** the Center for Peace, Nonviolence and Human Rights has used Listening Projects as the foundation for

their successful post war reconciliation work in six ethnically divided communities. Peace Teams of four to six members working in each community have used their Listening Projects to build positive relations and successful programs for peace and community development.

> *"It was remarkable. I was talking to a man who has been a major antagonist against the Muslims in Brestovac and then after I really listened to him he was willing to support peacemaking efforts."*
>
> Ildiko Erdei,
> Pancevo Peace Movement

RSVP's **Facilitated Dialogue** utilizes the same principles as the Listening Project. It focuses on listening within **small groups** of people having different or opposing beliefs (rather than listening through individual interviews). Trained facilitators as well as contractual guidelines and other structures help insure a communication environment based on compassion, deep listening and mutual respect.

Contact Information:
Rural Southern Voice for Peace
1898 Hannah Branch Rd.
Burnsville, North Carolina, U.S.A. 28714
Phone: (828) 675-5933
E-Mail: rsvp028714@yahoo.com

CHAPTER 13

THE JEWISH/PALESTINIAN LIVING ROOM DIALOGUE GROUP

There are things that governments can do that people cannot —

writing and fulfilling treaties. But treaties are just cold pieces of paper.

What citizens can do is change the nature of relationships.

Lionel Traubman

Jews and Palestinians living here are different from the ones living there,

where there's so much tension. But we are at least making an effort. I say, don't lose hope.

There's always hope.

Nahida Salem

(Written by organizing members of the Jewish/ Palestinian Living Room Dialogy Group)

We are 30 Americans. Among us are Holocaust survivors and 20th-generation Palestinians. ...We saw how face-to-face dialogue changes people. Realizing that American citizens and government are connected to events in the Middle East, it was time to put our global experience to use in our community.

In Spring, 2002, after 9 years together, the Jewish-Palestinian Living Room Dialogue Group of San Mateo County, CA, was preparing for its 123rd meeting. What follows is the limited, still-unfolding experience of a few participants — citizens who believe that the individual makes a difference.

FREQUENTLY ASKED QUESTIONS: PALESTINIAN-JEWISH DIALOGUE

WHAT IS DIALOGUE?

The purpose of true dialogue is to change the nature of relationships. It is not discussion or

debate, or even conflict resolution. Beginning with compassionate listening, it is offering a window to one's own thoughts, mental models, and heart, giving the other person a view into your life experience, reasoning, and humanity. With new, diverse ideas in the midst, and with a spirit of goodwill, divergent views can converge to un-cover a new social intelligence for the good of all.

Dialogue is described at http://www.igc.org/ traubman/dialogue.htm.

WHY DID YOU GET INVOLVED?

We began a dialogue group in July, 1992, because our life experience revealed that nothing replaces successful face-to-face relationships. Government peace processes were repeatedly failing. Most Jews and Palestinians had never had in-depth relationships nor heard anything but their own narratives, their own stories. Decisions — mostly bad decisions — continued to be made based on stereotypes and half-truths — ignorance. Creativ-ity, correcting stereotypes, and discovering trustworthy knowledge was not going to come from governments alone, but only with the help of citizens in true dialogue starting with one of the great acts of love — Compassionate Listening.

HOW DID YOU START?

We began with an idea. Then we found a Palestinian partner. Together we gathered enough women and men for a first meeting — 8-10 willing Jews and Palestinians, and a few "others." We phoned people we knew and those we didn't. We walked into places of business and introduced ourselves. And we returned and returned again to potential participants until they said "no" or walked through the front door into the dialogue experience. In time, the Palestinian and Jewish participants began opening their own living rooms for the monthly meetings, and we now limit the number to about 30. When new groups start now, it can help to invite in a few "seed" participants from an established dialogue.

WHAT ABOUT THOSE WHO ARE NEITHER PALESTINIANS NOR JEWS?

These "others," as they call themselves, have been important to our success. They moderate, encourage, and catalyze the dialogue. Their support has been a great contribution.

WHAT DID YOU DO WHEN YOU FIRST MET?

We introduced ourselves to one another. Many times. We listened to one another's personal stories and life views, at ever-deepening levels of understanding. Some were more quiet, cautious and protected. Some were assertive to the extreme - clinging to anger and hurt - and unable to hear others or focus on anything but their cause and view. We all shared one common interest for sure - food.

DID YOU HAVE A FACILITATOR?

After several meetings, we collectively chose to have a facilitator. In our case, a participant-attorney and mediator, neither Palestinian nor Jew, volunteered. He was excellent — a lion tamer at times — and deserves much of the credit for the success of our sustained endeavor. Even before choosing to have a facilitator, the group made its own agreements about preferred meeting times and places, hosting, and standards for being on time, listening, and courtesy — translate that to "interrupting each other."

WHAT WAS THE TONE OF THE FIRST MEETINGS?

First meetings can be either courteous or confronting. Each group has a different nature or personality. It is important to make room for flaring, especially when people have been holding their stories within for years, longing to be heard. This is where the others begin to master deep listening.

WHAT KIND OF COMMITMENT IS NEEDED?

Meaningful dialogue is "sustained dialogue." It truly is a process and takes dedication and time. Successful dialogue cannot be a passing fancy or hobby. It must be a preoccupation. Commitment to each other and to the process is important, as in any relationship.

WHY DO PEOPLE LEAVE A DIALOGUE GROUP?

People come in for different reasons. Some are quite process-oriented and would simply talk forever; some seek collective "action" and even political statements and stands "now." In our experience, especially in the beginning, people came and then left out of disinterest or impatience, or because they were too busy or didn't think the activity would make a difference. Some were afraid of judgment from within their own cultural, religious, or spiritual communities. Some could not open themselves up to hear any but their own narratives. Some simply sought allies for their cause. In time, for us, a devoted base developed and stayed. Through time, some participants have decided to discontinue, and others have entered the dialogue anew, and with appreciation and enthusiasm.

HOW DOES DIALOGUE CHANGE PEOPLE AND AFFECT POLITICAL OUTCOMES?

When we hear each other's "stories," we start to expand our identification, and begin to see each other as human and equal. Seeing our oneness — and differences, as well — we begin to want the best for each other. We see that we are inextricably interrelated and interdependent — neighbors forever. If enough citizens begin to have this experience, it will make the environment fertile and right for the government peace process to go to completion.

HOW DO YOU THINK DIALOGUE IN NORTH AMERICA MAKES A DIFFERENCE?

We can have an important affect on the Middle East, through our government's diplomatic, military, and economic policies. We can also contribute useful perceptions and even wisdom, being at a distance from the emotional centers of conflict. Perhaps most important is our tradition of freedom and creativity with which we can discover new models of thinking and treating one other. Many of us have family and friends in Israel/Palestine to whose thinking and spirit we can contribute, especially with the help of telephone and Internet communication, and a Web site.

IN DIALOGUE, WHAT IS THE "ACTION"?

The action of dialogue is building relationships, and expanding the circle of people who engage in that activity.

WHAT ABOUT THOSE WHO PREFER MORE POLITICAL ACTIVISM?

In time, individuals who begin to identify with a larger frame of reference may choose to express themselves differently and more publicly. But the true "action" is to widen the circle of relationships in which former enemies expand their identification and begin to want the best for each other. Then, political outcomes that serve both peoples equally are more likely to go to completion. Other kinds of expressions about positions, statements, and causes are also important. But they do not correct stereotypes and fundamental attitudes of people toward each other. This is the function of dialogue.

CAN A DIALOGUE PARTICIPANT REPRESENT A GROUP OR INSTITUTION?

Each participant enters dialogue as an individual speaking only for herself or himself, free from any attachments to other people or groups. Attachment to the positions, interests, or judgment of a whole collective removes the freedom needed for authentic individual participation. It is helpful for people in leadership to acknowledge their affiliations, and simply do the very best they can in dialogue.

WHEN DID YOU DO YOUR FIRST PUBLIC OUTREACH ACTIVITY?

We did not do any kind of public outreach for over a year and a half, because we didn't feel we had anything to say until then. We needed time to build trust and to learn, enabling our outreach to be successful. Any earlier action would have been "skipping steps" in the relationship-building public peace process.

See http://www.igc.org/traubman/pubpeace.htm.

HOW DO YOU RESPOND IN TIMES OF CRISIS?

When your peoples and their governments are in trying times — violence, disarray, perturbation — the most important thing is to be there for each other. Do not withdraw from one other. People's expectations may not be met, but it is better to at least share your common humanity — both pain and hopes — and widen the circle of those who can begin to identify with each other, than to allow the continuation of the awful stereotypes that push around and paralyze both peoples, in America and in the Middle East.

JEWISH/PALESTINIAN LIVINGROOM DIALOGUE PROJECTS

In July, 1992, here on the San Francisco peninsula, as part of a larger public peace process we invited American Palestinians and Jews to begin a long-term dialogue together to discover common ground and improve the environment for reconciliation here in America.

Today we are about 20 Palestinians and Jews, and 10 "others." Many participants have come and gone from our group, taking the experience with them.

In 2001, after 104 meetings and eight years, we have moved from caution to integrity, from alienation to familiarity, from ignorance to understanding, from confrontation to collaboration. As a result, we have:

• Learned about listening, integrity, persistence, and dedication.

• Written joint letters to leaders in the United States and the Middle East, including over 90 leaders and opinion formers in Washington. The final contents of these messages were hard-won after much conflict, dialogue, then agreement, before we all placed our signatures.

• Attended synagogue together, and placed a ground-breaking display of Palestinian art in a local temple.

• Participated in our local Palestinian Cultural Days, and presented an educational table to inform and invite new Palestinians to participate.

• Given public introductory presentations for new people. Typically 50-80 attendees sit at round tables, eating home-made Palestinian and Jewish food and becoming acquainted. Several of us give talks about our personal dialogue group experiences, before the people at tables began moderated, sample dialogues of their own.

• Helped the local Israeli Consulate, at their invitation, with recent Jewish-Palestinian cultural activities which they have begun to initiate.

• Sent $1,300 cash and $20,000 worth of medical equipment to help two hospitals, one in Gaza, and another in western Jerusalem.

• Helped launch three new "spin-off" dialogue groups here in the Bay Area.

• Been interviewed on a local television talk show for 30 minutes about the history, principles, and activities of our dialogue group and about the public peace process.

• Raised $10,000 for schools in need, equally, in Netanya, Israel and Ramallah, Palestine. For their part, the two faculties began meeting in their own new face-to-face dialogue process.

• Co-sponsored an educational fundraising event for Neve Shalom/Wahat al-Salam (Oasis of Peace), a model village where Jews and Palestinians live and learn together. Two hundred attended.

• Published editorial articles "On Passover and Peace" and "To Build a Common Future" and "A Missing Step in the Peace Process" in major metropolitan newspapers.

• Sponsored "Building A Common Future", a historic, relationship-building dinner near San Francisco for 420 Jewish and Palestinian Americans, and others, to begin changing the nature of their relationships and invigorate the public peace process. About 100 attendees signed up to continue with in-home mealsharing groups.

• Recorded a radio interview for the international broadcast of "Unofficial Channels: Dialogue for Middle East Peace," by the National Radio Project.

• Provided a guest panel for University of California, Santa Cruz, students' first "Jewish-Palestinian Dialogue Workshop."

• Helped educate high school classes studying Palestinian-Jewish conflicts and the value of dialogue in the public peace process.

• Presented a workshop on dialogue, trialogue, and conflict resolution to teen "Future Leaders of the Jewish Community." (Syllabus available upon request.)

• Assisted a synagogue Friday evening dedicated to peace — Jewish-Palestinian dinner, Shabbos services, exhibits, and panel presentation.

• Helped the 1998 San Francisco Jewish Film Festival with audience development for their North American premier of "AL NAKBA: The Palestinian Catastrophe 1948."

• Provided a "Lunch and Learn" program for the Montefiore Senior Center of the Jewish Community Center.

• Helped YES! Magazine publish an article, "Living Room Dialogues."

• Held a quilting workshop to create squares for the travelling Middle East Peace Quilt of Elizabeth Shefrin, Vancouver, Canada, a fabric artist who teaches "Stitching for Social Change."

• Co-sponsored with the World Affairs Council a public presentation for 350 by M.K. Dr. Yossi Beilin and Palestinian leader Faisal al-Husseini.

• Provided an interview about our Palestinian-Jewish dialogue process for Planetary Dialogues on the Internet.

• Sponsored and facilitated the First All-Bay-Area Meeting of Jewish-Palestinian Living Room Dialogue Groups.

• Participated as panelists in "Dialogue Is Action," a 1999 conference of Stanford University, Office of Multicultural Education.

• Helped financial donors identify worthy projects that join Palestinians and Jews in dialogue, and in activities that help change enemies into partners.

• Mailed dialogue guidelines and relationship-building ideas to over 810 individuals, including 520 institutions, 350 cities, 38 states, and 29 countries.

• Used the Internet to forward encouraging news about successful Palestinian-Jewish collaboration, here and in the Middle East.

• Organized a Spring dinner-ceremony: "A Celebration of Freedom for All the Children of Abraham, Hagar, and Sarah."

• Helped students in high schools, universities, and graduate studies, by providing printed materials and personal interviews about principles and results of citizen relationship-building.

• Celebrated our Third Annual Jewish-Palestinian Dinner in May, 2000 with music and dancing from both cultures, equally.

• Helped a new San Francisco Dialogue Group get launched then, after two years, co-sponsored with the Jewish Community Center an evening Reception for 100 Arabs and Jews.

• Provided media interviews, during the Fall, 2000, violent outbreaks, for local newspapers, radio, and TV, for CNN, and for Canadian radio, to communicate alternative ways of thinking and responding.

• Helped a new dialogue group to begin in Silicon Valley, despite Middle East violence.

• Offered program development assistance for the Christian Science Sentinel - Radio Edition broadcast, "Common ground for peace-building in the Middle East."

• Provided a panel for a November, 2000 "Teens-only Middle East Forum" sponsored by the Jewish Community Center of San Francisco at the request of youth to expand their views.

• Spoke at "Coming Together to Bridge Racial Differences," a community forum sponsored in part by the National Education Association.

Contact Information:
Jewish/Palestinian Living Room Dialogue Group
1448 Cedarwood Dr.
San Mateo, CA 94403
Voice (650) 574-8303 Fax (650) 573-1217
Web: http://traubman.igc.org
E-mail: LTRAUBMAN@igc.org

APPENDIX

ADDITIONAL EXERCISES

The additional exercises presented in this section follow the Preparation Outline which follows. They come from many sources; some are original. Many can be adapted for individual preparation as well as for groups. I encourage you to develop your own to fit your purposes and the needs of the group. Remember that some groups and some individuals within groups are uncomfortable with deep, internal processes. Imagery and energy exercises are not appropriate in these cases. People should always be given the option to not participate and/or do so in their own way. Imagining with eyes open is one way of adapting a meditation-type process. And writing is another option to sharing with another person or in a small group.

There are numerous group facilitation books and manuals available in book stores from which you can adapt exercises. However, in my experience, I have found less to be more.

It is important to allow time with each experience for people to process deeply and have ample time to integrate the lessons. Writing down their experiences and responses is a valuable first step.

Often it is helpful to share with one or two people in depth before presenting to the whole group. If you limit sharing to small groups, the whole body may miss the integration which comes from everyone being witness to the experiences of others. On the other hand, the large group process sometimes intimidates people, while sharing with a small group encourages an opening. A leader has to weigh all these factors when planning.

One must also be open to the unexpected. Whereas people feel confidence in a leader who keeps to an agenda, there are times when some-

thing does come up which needs addressing. Leadership means using discretion. I find that being transparent with the whole group about such decisions serves as a model and also engenders cooperation. This is a personal style. I've seen it done many ways.

PREPARATION

OUTLINE
1. Creating a Safe Container
2. Introductions
3. Team Building
4. Vision
5 . Centering Practices
6. Listening with a "Greater" Mind and Heart
7. Formulating Compassionate Questions
8. Strategic Questioning
9. Reflective Listening
10. Taking Charge of Emotions
11. Grounding New Learnings With Imagery
12. Closing

1. CREATING A SAFE CONTAINER

- Introduce yourself.
- Acknowledge and appreciate the people who have shown up.
- Dedicate the gathering to the greatest good.
- Explain briefly the purpose of the meeting as you understand it.
- State your understanding of your role as leader
- Develop group guidelines
- Ripen awareness of silence and timing
- Ask people to briefly name where they are from, their involvement with the issue, their desired outcome for this group experience.

2. INTRODUCTIONS

General Introduction:

Briefly state your name, where you are from, your involvement with the issue, and your desired outcome for this group experience.

Connecting to Group

A volunteer time keeper assures everyone an equal, predetermined time. People go around the circle answering the question: "Why I am here?" This simple question allows the choice of what to say about themselves and to connect themselves to the purpose of the group. Sometimes we have been more explicit about the question: "What brought you here?"
"How does this trip relate to your life?"
"What are your concerns?"

These questions open up common goals and background which connect people with each other.

3. TEAM BUILDING

Ball Toss

This activity can be helpful to interact with other members of the group or can serve as a way to bring up the energy if people have been listening a long time. Twelve people is maximum. If the group is larger, others can engage by observing and offering suggestions for problem solving. Anyone familiar with the game should not participate or coach but could act as timekeeper.

The purpose is to build team problem-solving skills by passing a ball to each other in a repeatable way, and in the shortest possible time. A tennis ball and a second hand time piece are needed.

Have the four directions written out and visible to the group:
- Each person gets the ball once
- Must touch the ball with two hands
- Only one person at a time touches the ball which is passed in the same order each time
- Ball cannot touch the ground

For the first two rounds have people say the name of the person to whom they are throwing the ball as they throw it.

The last person in the sequence keeps the ball and then hands it back to the first person to repeat the sequence.

After the third round, the leader times the sequence from the initiation until the last person receives the ball. Leader mentions it is possible to cut the time in half.

After each sequence, the leader asks if it isn't possible to do it even faster. The timing will challenge the group to find creative ways to speed up the process. A group of ten can do it in approximately two seconds.

Complex, Adaptive, Self Organizing Systems (CASOS)

People are usually uncomfortable with chaos. This exercise shows that ultimately, group chaos will resolve itself through its own self-organization.

It is quite reassuring to realize there seems to be an order extant in the universe, working itself into our awareness.

Each person:
- Mentally identifies two other people without indicating who they are
- Keeps equidistant from the two s/he has picked (not necessarily in an equilateral triangle)

The group will begin to move around in different patterns and ultimately come to a stop when everyone is equidistant from the two people they identified. When the movement ceases, allow people time to discuss the implications.

4. VISION

Clarifying Purpose

When forming a study group, it's important to clarify the purpose of all the individuals and to be clear what everyone wants from the group process.

This clarifying meditation can be drawn, and/or written, and then shared with the group.

Close your eyes and relax. Be conscious of your breath. Allow enough time in silence to sink into a deep state of relaxation. Allow an image/sense/symbol of the meaning for you of Compassionate Listening. Explore that for yourself.

Be aware of the higher qualities you bring as an individual to this collective process. Image and sense your relationship to the whole (archetype) of Compassionate Listening. Be aware of your feelings as you allow yourself to be a part of this image. Be aware of the other people in the room who share a similar attraction to this image. Imagine this group manifesting the qualities and energies of Compassionate Listening. Perhaps the image/sense will grow and change. What is emerging?

Take a deep breath and bring your awareness back to yourself sitting in the chair. Feel your feet on the ground and slowly open your eyes, silently acknowledging yourself and the others in the room.

Draw/write about your image in silence. Share your image with the group and explore where you are now in relation to this ideal ; what growth do you know you wish to make; and what resources do you have within which will contribute to your own growth and that of the group?

Values Clarification

In this exercise, you can find clarity on the issues and things that are really important to you. You will find where your passions lie. It also illustrates underlying interests, needs and concerns.

Make a list on the left hand side of a piece of paper of no more than ten things which bring you pleasure in your life and hold meaning for you. They can be as mundane as your love of ice cream to bigger issues of creating community or walking in the woods or world peace.

When you have listed ten or so things, think of the qualities or energy which are evoked when you are engaged in these things. For example, the love of ice cream may mean indulgence, permission, celebration. A walk in the woods may mean relaxation, freedom, health, spirituality. Creating community may mean love, sharing, cooperation. You may find that many of the same qualities appear on the list for different reasons.

On a second piece of paper, make a list on the left hand side of ten things which upset you. For example, nuclear proliferation, crowded airports, muddy footprints on the carpet. Then ask yourself, what quality or energy is missing for me that I get upset by this? Nuclear proliferation may mean the quality of health, safety, freedom are at stake. Crowded airports may mean freedom, balance, and serenity are missing. Muddy footprints again may mean freedom, or being honored, or a sense of order and beauty are missing.

Review the qualities from both lists. If you really give thought to these two simple lists, you can get a very good idea of the qualities of life which have deep meaning for you. This exercise also points out that things are not necessarily what they appear to be. Issues that may seem simple can be connected to qualities that have tremendous energy and meaning. This energy may motivate you to seek out projects which connect to these issues, or they may be a caution to approach such issues carefully. They may be too important to you to put aside your own biases in order to be present to others.

"Don't do something. Just sit there."

title of a book on meditation
by Judith Boornstein

5. CENTERING PRACTICES

• The facilitator asks what practices individuals already use which help them when they become stressed.

• People share what they do in their lives to center themselves as a part of their introduction.

• Focus your attention on your breath. A very fundamental practice is to say to yourself: "I am breathing in light and releasing darkness."

• A variation on the above is to imagine breathing in the darkness around you, transducing it to light energy, and releasing it to others as light.

• When you find yourself upset and/or distracted, connect viscerally with body sensations. Identify the feeling and consciously release it.

• Grounding/ re-energizing:
Sit in a chair, with your feet flat on the floor and only your hands on your lap. Close your eyes. Slowly imagine roots starting at the base of your spine and going down through your chair, through the floor, through the foundation of this building, into the earth, and continuing down to a solid place in the earth where they can be strongly attached in whatever way you like. Make sure your roots begin at the base of your spine and not at your forehead! Now breathe and allow all the events and thoughts of the day, positive and negative, to be funneled through your roots and to be absorbed into the earth. Now do the same with the major events of the past week. Notice some events or thoughts may not want to leave, and realize that you can call them back at any time. Release them, with your breath, into your roots and into the earth. Once you have learned this, you can ground yourself at any time.

Now breathe new, clean earth energy up through your roots. Allow it slowly to fill your feet, legs, and the lower half of your trunk. Now allow your highest pale gold or white energy to funnel into your body through the center of the top of your head, slowly filling the top part of your body and mixing with the earth energy in the lower part of your body. Allow the mixture to swirl through your entire body, adjusting it with your breathing, so you feel neither too light headed; nor too heavy. When you are ready, bend over, let the energy go, give yourself a shake and open your eyes.

• Angel Cards are commercially available: a small deck of cards with higher qualities depicted such as efficiency, transformation, trust, responsibility, beauty, understanding, and many more. We have asked people to draw a card for each session and be responsible for holding that quality for the whole group.

• If people are comfortable with energy practices, be acutely aware of the other person while you are listening. This is considered holding their energy and is a gift to them. It's really the essence of Compassionate Listening.

• When you are upset, focus your attention for a few seconds on a beautiful object anywhere in your environment.

• When information raises emotions, support yourself and others in a field of compassion. You might imagine everyone being held in a chalice of soft light.

• Visualize your mind as a calm, deep lake with very still water. As you look into the lake you see a beautiful reflection of a snow capped mountain. Imagine that your thoughts are the winds which cause the ripples on the surface and prevent your seeing the reflection clearly. As your thoughts slow down, the reflection becomes clearer. Breathe deeply and calm your mind by concentrating on the beauty and stillness of the lake.

6. LISTENING WITH A GREATER MIND AND HEART

The Value of Listening:

Remember back to a time when you were listened to compassionately. What was that like for you?

Now remember a time when you were not listened to. How was that for you?

Remember a time when you listened to someone else with your full attention.

Now recall a time when you did not listen to someone. How was that for you and the other person?

Write these insights and/or share with a partner.

Extrapolate the essence/qualities/energies of compassionate, deep listening.

Make a list of the positive qualities of CL and another list of what can be the negative effects of poor listening. People often bring up the following:

Positive - balance, expansion, engaged, beauty, focus, connection, calmness, understanding, peace, potential, smiling, all senses, flow, see the facets of the whole.

Negative - competition, chaos, aggression, fiery barrier, need to be right, self-centered, shut-down, time, vulnerability, darkness, feeling small, fear, structured, confusion, personal agendas, bias.

Write about or discuss these aspects.

7. HEALING INTERNAL CHAOS

I was introduced to these exercises many years ago in my Psychosynthesis training in San Francisco. The purpose is to become aware of patterns, to make a choice of what best serves us, and to integrate the conflicts to a new way of being. They point out how a disturbance "out there" is a reflection of a disturbance within.

In Psychosynthesis, these "voices" are referred to as subpersonalities — many parts of ourselves who make up our personality. In this exercise, the center of the circle represents the "Self," or "Center" of the personality system which regulates the many aspects of our being.

These particular exercises can be raucous if the assigned voices get into their parts. They can be very moving, often bringing us to tears when we realize how hard we are on ourselves: acknowledging the many wars we carry within us. For many, the most difficult part of these exercises is letting the good parts speak lovingly to us. Opening to our inner goodness is often the most difficult of inner work. Allow 10-15 minutes for each person's process.

Purpose:
• To recognize the parts within ourselves which are in conflict.
• To acknowledge the positive and helpful aspects of these parts.
• To experience the empowerment which comes from unleashing their positive aspects and energies and directing them in ways which serve our present interests.

These exercises allow us to hear some of our own judgements and have the opportunity to experience how that feels and how it feels to change the messages. They demonstrate how much of our conflict is internal.

Circle of Parts

Take about 5 minutes to think about your major judgmental inner voices – think of 2 or 3 dominant voices that play inside your head. What are these judgements – what are the specific words? Write these down in your journal. (Use "you" in your phrasing… so that it's clear these are not your true identity.)

(Ask for a volunteer to demonstrate the exercise with the whole group)

Step #1: Person assigns roles to two or three people of his/her major inner voices, giving each person a brief scenario of how that voice tends to operate and what it might say. Remember to give instructions about the tone – is the voice meek or loud?

Step #2: Person stands in center of circle and listens to the assigned people verbalize the voices all at one time. Experience what it is like to be bombarded by all these voices. What does it feel like? Body? Feeling? Is this what it is like in life sometimes? Be aware of the stress. Respond however you'd like to respond. There are no rules.

Step #3: When you are ready, move outside the circle and observe the voices as they continue to speak. What do you see? What do you learn?

(Instruct group not to stop the action too quickly at this point – really take it in.)

Step #4. Stop the action. Experience the power of saying "no" to the bombardment. Move back into the circle and quiet yourself. Find your "center" by breathing and feeling your feet firmly planted on the floor. Come to a state of balance by noticing the relaxation of leg and feet muscles; muscles around chest and abdomen. Breathe deeply. Take enough time for this step. Experience the quiet within.

Step #5. Now transform those negative messages one by one, by giving each a positive voice. Tell each where they came from in your life. Realize they developed as a way of helping you survive a difficult situation. Feel appreciation for what they have given you in your life. Their energy became blocked at that point in time and they didn't develop with the rest of you. Tell each what their positive side is and tell them how they can support you and how you can support them now. Let the people in the circle take on those positive voices. Let them verbalize how they can support you. Let each give you positive feedback and let you know how they appreciate you and help you. Thank each one and tell it what it does to hinder or block you and what positive aspects it has as well. Keep bringing this into your body, notice your breath and your feet on the ground. (Again, encourage people not to stop this phase too quickly.)

Debrief

This exercise continues as each person moves to the center and assigns the rest of the group his/her subpersonalities.

Get into groups of 4 and let everyone have this experience. Make sure the person who volunteered is in one of the largest groups since he/she won't need to do it again.

Voice Dialog Exercises

These exercises are similar to "Voice Dialogue", a therapy system developed by Hal and Sidra Stone, having its roots in Psychosynthesis subpersonality work.

There are three exercises here. The first set of questions can be done alone while writing in a journal. The questions can also be asked with two people working together. One person should complete the whole exercise before changing roles. The facilitator asks all the questions and the person working moves from one chair to another to represent each inner voice. Then they switch roles. The third section can be done as a *Dance of the Selves*. They can all be done separately or they can build on one another.

SECTIONS ONE and TWO
1. Sit quietly and reflect on your major judgements against yourself. They may appear around a particular inner conflict or a conflict which you face in your life. Identify the voices within you which hold you captive and demean you, criticize you, condemn you, evaluate you, and cause you pain. Make a list of them without details. Just identify them and list them.

2. Look over your list and pick two of the strongest ones. Identify each voice. Give each a name. You are going to establish a dialogue with each voice and then teach them to work together with you. Work with one first and write their answers as they speak to you. When complete with one, stand up and shake off that identity. Then start with the second voice. Ask the following questions as though they were separate people and write THEIR answers.

- What brings you out?
- When you show up in my life, what is it you are trying to do for me?
- What do you need?
- What are your deeper concerns?
- How do you feel about me?
- When did you come in to my life and for what purpose? How did you develop?
- I am beginning to appreciate what you have tried to do for me. You came into my life as a way of helping me through some tough times. How do you see we could get along better now?
- You hold value for me. I need to use your energy properly in my life. I want you to ………

3. When you have completed both conversations, move and breathe. Shake them off and Center yourself. Now from your deeper self, reflect upon what they have both said.

- Have you come to a win/win place? If not, what more is needed?
- Identify your common interests, needs and concerns.
- Appreciate how much they have been there for you.
- Write down the changes you want to see happen and how you can utilize and engage their energy in helping you do this. Look for ways you can integrate them in to your life in a positive, helpful way. Your conflict with them has dissipated the useful energy they hold in potential for you. Take charge now and use it in a positive way.

4. Reflect upon these voices you have come to know and appreciate.
- Have they been working negatively in your attitude toward others, as well? Do you hold the same judgements for others as you do for yourself?
- How can this internal reconciliation reflect in your relationships with others? You may want to take notes on these reflections.

When these steps are complete you can add the following movements as a way of integrating your new understanding.

SECTION THREE
1. Stand with a space of three feet in all directions. Where you are now standing is your place of Center. The place of witness and neutral observer.

Close your eyes and feel yourself as grounded with energy connecting from your feet in to the earth.   Breathe deeply.
- With your eyes closed imagine one of your judgmental parts standing forward in a circle on your right and the other forward in a circle on your left. See them as personalities, first one and then the other.
- What do they look like? How are they dressed? What size are they? What colors are they wearing? What do you sense about them?
- Step in to one of the circles now and become that part. Put on the attitudes and feelings as though it were a costume. Become that part now. Let it have a voice. Think its thoughts, feel its feelings, exaggerate its physical stance. Let your body go in to a position and hold it for a moment so you can remember it.
- What does the situation look like to you in this place? How does the world look? What would your life be like if you were this part all the time?
- What does this part of you want? What does it want of you? Of the situation? What does it say? Go deeper. What does this part need? What is its essence? What qualities does it express in you. What qualities does it need to develop?
- Now move back in to the center position from which you came – the place of the witness and neutral observer. Shake off the patterns you have been holding. From this neutral position in the middle, look back at it. Can you understand that part and even feel some compassion for its position? If you are experiencing judgement, then step in to a new circle. This Center Circle is reserved for a neutral observer. The new judgement may be another part of your internal conflict. Then consciously step back to the Center position and see if you can be an observer.
- From this neutral place, become aware of another part of this internal conflict.

Step in to another circle and repeat what you did with the first part. Become it, take on its position and ask it the questions.

• Step back in to the center and shake it off. Breathe and center yourself. Look at this second part? Can you do so with understanding and compassion?

• Let the two parts dialogue with each other. Step in to each circle as they speak. Step in to the Center and have a three-way dialogue. What do they want from each other? What do they feel when the other is in control? When they are in control?

• As you dialogue, you may come upon yet another part. Create another space and develop this character in the same way.

• Step back in to the center and observe the whole spectrum. Can you experience yourself observing without being caught in it? If feelings come up about it, center yourself. Notice if there is any resolution between the parts? Is there anything more that they need to say to each other? Move from one circle in to the others. This movement can become a dance which can be speeded up ultimately, eliminating the need for words. Enjoy the "still point of the moving world" and the transformation which comes from the movement – from becoming "unstuck."

• Now take a moment to go deep inside your self. This is your place of empowerment – that of knowing your can handle these conflicts positively and be in control. Get in touch with your vision of peace, of peace at all levels. What is your choice? See yourself utilizing these qualities and the pure essence of these parts of you to move forward with your choice. Notice, recognize and love these aspects of yourself that had divergent outlooks.

• Realize the creativity when they work together. Appreciate yourself for your vision and your intention. When you become aware of the conflicts of those parts, acknowledge their presence, embrace them and move on with your choices.

Roleplay of "Listening Do's & Don'ts"
Purpose is to bring awareness to poor listening habits and the shift to effective listening habits.

One leader share a problem. Other leader demonstrates key ways not to listen such as:
    interrupting
    interrogating
    sharing own problem
    minimizing
    judging
    giving advice

Ask for group response and their identification of what was wrong and what needed to be done instead.

Leader then shares the same problem and other leader demonstrates effective Listening Do's"- including the following:
    reflect
    acknowledge
    support
    encourage
    positive body language
    clarify

Again ask for group response. Get group to identify the components of good listening. Group can break into dyads and practice the good listening skills.

8. INQUIRY

These quotes and questions, compiled by Gene Knudsen Hoffman, are especially appropriate for an introduction of a group and when people are having difficulty getting through positions:

Perhaps everything terrible is, in its deepest being, something that needs our love.
               Rainer Maria Rilke

• Have you known someone or something 'terrible' that needs your love? Can you tell us about it?
• Did loving him/her/it change you? How?

We must love them both, those whose opinions we share, and those whose opinions we reject, for both have labored in the search for truth, and both have helped us in the finding of it.

Thomas Aquinas

- Have you ever loved someone with whom you deeply disagreed on almost everything important to you? Tell us about it.
- Did you, or can you now find an area of commonality between you and that person? Can you tell us about it?
- Did you learn to love that person? Tell us about that and the kind of love you discovered.

9. STRATEGIC QUESTIONING

Strategic questions can be helpful to steer the person to the subject we have come to hear: namely, their personal experience of the situation they are in.

Fran Peavey talks about strategic questioning and makes some useful points:
"Shaping a strategic question involves seven key features. A strategic question:
- Creates motion,
- Creates options,
- Digs deeper,
- Avoids "why",
- Avoids "yes or no" answers,
- Is empowering,
- Asks the unaskable questions (those which challenge the values and assumptions that the whole issue rests upon).

An important task of strategic questioning is to create an environment where people can see the solutions that are within themselves. You listen deeply into the moving heart of the person opposite you. A strategic questioner listens for the latent solutions hidden within every problem. And this involves a special type of listening. You are not passively listening. You are creating an action path with your attention.

(Excerpt adapted from *By Life's Grace: Musings on the Essence of Social Change* by Fran Peavey.)

The following questions are offered as food for thought. They are most appropriate when mediating a conflict. Some are appropriate for a listening session. They can serve as guides should a conflict erupt during a listening session and for further problem solving sessions which might occur subsequent to a listening session.

Stimulating/creating options in a conflict:

- How can you address this situation in a way that provides for A's need for x, B's need for y, and Their common needs of z?
- If you were to describe two acceptable options, what would they be?
- Are there other ways to solve this problem?
- If (money) were not an issue here, how might you resolve....?
- If A were willing to do x, might you be willing to do y?
- If you were B now, what do you think might work for him/her?
- Can any of you think of an option which hasn't been mentioned yet?

Breaking impasse:

- If you were a most wise fly on the wall, what do you think might work?
- Five years from now, looking back, what agreement would have worked?
- I know you and B cannot agree, but if you were to agree, what might that look like?
- If A wants her way, and B wants his, can you imagine a third way that might work for both of you? If you are to agree, both of you will have to change. Think about what you might be willing to change.

Addressing Rank as Americans:

- How are we as Americans using/abusing our position?
- How do Palestinian Muslims and Christians see us as Americans, as Jews? as Arab Americans, as Christians, as secular?
- How do Israelis see us?
- What privileges are connected in these instances?

Bringing out the marginalized parts of our own selves:

Victim, oppressor, religious, secular, wasp, Jew, Muslim, male, female, leader, follower; culturally acceptable, internalized outsider, youth, elder, economic, social class.

• How have you been oppressed in your life?
• How have you oppressed others?
• What does that feel like in both instances?
• How do you feel about others in both instances?
• What is the source of your courage?
• We hear the injustice and the pain. What would it take for you to put your hatred behind you?

Questions of Curiosity, Questions that Connect
Developed by Joy Helmer, MS

Time: 45 minutes for the exercise, 15 minutes large group debriefing.

This exercise was designed to practice formulating questions which penetrate the wall of resistance between the questioner and the person being questioned. Joy has used it as practice for people listening to prisoners in a maximum facility prison. It can be useful in training for learning how to reach out to people who mistrust us and offer strong resistance to any relationship. It will bring up strong feelings and will give you good practice in setting emotions aside in order to ask questions of curiosity and questions that connect and to experience the difference. This is a powerful exercise.

Demonstrate this process in front of the group first.

Step 1. Divide into groups of 5 or 6.

Step 2. Each person in the group will, over the course of the exercise, have an opportunity to take each of three roles: that of person asking questions, that of person receiving and experiencing the questions, and scribe.

Step 3. The attached scenarios are de-

signed to bring up strong feelings for the questioners. You may decide as a group to use only one scenario for all participants throughout the time of the exercise. Or you may experiment with different scenarios in different rounds. The scribe will write the questions down so that everyone will remember them. The group will rotate so that each person gets to be the question receiver, question asker and scribe.

Step 4. *Question Receiver:* You will be playing the part of an offender who has committed an act of severe violence. Try to imagine what the inner world of such a person might be like. The other members will take turns asking questions of you. Do not reply to them. Remain silent and notice the effects inside you of each question. Does the questions make you think? Does it make you want to open up or close down? You will be especially calling on the skill of body focusing here.

Step 5. *Question Askers:* Choose a scenario that brings up strong feelings inside you, perhaps of judgement, disgust, anger, rage, confusion. Notice those reactions inside your body. Then experiment with putting these emotions aside so that you can be present to the offender. Pause between each question asked so that the receiver can note the effect of the question. You may ask more than one question if you like but be careful about overwhelming the receiver with too many questions. Also, be aware of the time so that each person gets to ask questions, receive questions and act as scribe.

Step 6. *Scribe:* notes down each question. Give the questions to the receiver when the round of questions is done.

Step 7. After each person has asked questions the receiver can briefly tell the others the effect the various questions had on him/her. The purpose of this exercise is to experiment with various kinds of questions, striving for an attitude of genuine curiosity and looking for those kinds of questions that allow for connection and for something new to happen or to be learned.

Scenarios: One example is given here. Develop your own by creating really closed and difficult situations to roleplay which fit the situations in which you work.

The offender is a man in his mid-twenties convicted of a hate crime. He deliberately went to an area of town known to be frequented by male homosexuals, picked up a young man on a ruse, took him to an isolated area and beat him very severely. The victim survived but has severe brain damage. The offender has a long history of violence, starting in grade school with bullying, progressing to car thefts and assaults as a juvenile and culminating in the charge of attempted murder.

10. REFLECTIVE LISTENING

Sit with a partner. Think of something which was effective, positive and meaningful for you in your life or in this project. Speak to your partner for 3 minutes about it.

Listener responds with body language. When the speaker is complete, the listener lets the speaker know what s/he understood and the feelings reflected from what the speaker shared.
Change roles and repeat.

11. TAKING CHARGE OF EMOTIONS

Your Response to Anger
• When upset, find ways of grounding yourself. Feel your body sitting on the chair or imagine roots extending from your feet straight down into the earth. Breathe through these roots.
• Break into groups of 3 and discuss what makes you angry and how you respond: focus on one or two experiences.
Extrapolate the elements in large group.
Express anger through drawing: comfortable range to catastrophic expectations.
• Discussion
What does the anger protect? Is there fear and vulnerability? Is it useful? What is the value of expressing anger, if any? Is there a choice of expressing rather than reacting?

Transformation of Anger
Do you use anger as a way to intimidate others or to force your point of view?
Is anger an addiction? What are other possible responses?
What are the ways you can meet your needs as an alternative to anger?
What is the relationship of your anger to blame (self and other)?
How might you engage the skillful and good will i.e. Ghandi?
What are ways of optimizing the energy of anger?
What is the role of indignation?

Ideal Model
(Can be used in relation to anger, fear, listening, or any subject)
What is the way you think you should be when angry?
What is the worst way you fear you may be?
What is the way you think other people see you?
What might be the ideal and realistic way you can and choose to be?

Softening Anger Energy
Ask people to relax, attend to their breathing. Read the following quote:

When someone upsets you, you can go into what they are like and why they did it or you can go into what you are like and why it upsets you. It needs skill in stating your own feelings without making the problem worse. You can think of holding anger like a mother holding a baby. Just as the anger is inside of us, so is the lovingkindness of a mother holding a baby. So one part of us is taking care of another part. Every time the energy of anger is there, we should invite the energy of lovingkindness to be there to take care of the anger.

Thich Nhat Hanh in conversation with Ram Dass in *Inquiring Mind,: A Semi-Annual Journal of the Vipassana Community*, Vol 12, #3 Spring 1996

Transforming Emotions

This exercise is an adaptation of the Freeze Frame process developed by Doc Lew Childre of The Institute of HeartMath Discovery Program, Boulder Creek, CA.

Bring awareness to tension you are feeling or upsetting thoughts you may be having. Focus your attention on your heart. Breathe deeply through your heart, i.e., imagine your heart actually breathing in and out.

While continuing the breath in this way, remember a time when you felt calm, about a situation, or felt positive feelings toward a person, even the person who may be the source of your discomfort. Keep focussed on these positive feelings. Send that positive feeling to the person or situation and absorb it into yourself, as well.

Coming into Relationship with Anger

This exercise is from Thich Nhat Hanh in conversation with Ram Dass in *Inquiring Mind,: A Semi-annual Journal of the Vipassana Community*, Vol 12, #3 Spring 1996.

When you are breathing mindfully, you are not ignoring anger. In fact, you become mindful of your anger and take care of it. 'Breathing in, I know I am angry. Breathing out, I am taking good care of my anger.' If you continue like that for some time, there will be a transformation in the heart of anger. It's like the action of sunshine on the flowers. In the morning the flowers are not yet open, but the sunshine continues to visit. And the sunshine is not only circulating around the flowers, it is penetrating deeply into the flowers. If the sunshine continues like that for a few hours, then the flower has to open herself to the sunshine. Our anger is a kind of flower that needs the care of the sunshine of mindfulness.

Anger may be a source of energy, but when you are angry you are not lucid. You may say or do things that are destructive. That is why it's better to use the energy of compassion or the energy of understanding. People should know that the energy of anger can actually be transformed into the energy of understanding and compassion. We don't have to throw any energy away. We only need to know how to transform one form of energy into another.

12. GROUNDING NEW LEARNINGS WITH IMAGERY

Choosing Emotional Responses

Imagine yourself in an anger provoking situation and responding the way you would choose.

Reclaiming Projections

You can use this exercise as a visualization or as a dialogue. If working alone, you can write your dialogue, both your part and that of the other person. Or you can have three chairs, one for you, one for the image of the other person, and one for your "centered Self." The option of drawing images is also available.

Bring into your mind the image of a person who has been your severest teacher. Allow the feelings and emotions to surface. Visualize this person and even visualize some of the incidents which made these experiences severe. Have an imaginary dialogue with that person.

Now bring to your image a positive quality about that person. You may even need to imagine that person as an innocent child if your associations are severely negative. Can you open your heart to that person, as a child? As an adult? Send energy through your heart.

What are the gifts this person has ultimately brought to you? What did you learn by your association? How did this person strengthen and empower you?

I recall a variation of this exercise when a Jewish holocaust survivor was struggling with the image of her guards as her severest teacher. She had a terrible time coming to any positive gifts. And then she had an amazing breakthrough. She realized what a survivor she had become. She could have died and she hadn't — she had made a choice for life.

The Double Circle

This exercise has been adapted with permission from Joanna Macy, from her book, *Coming Back to Life: Practices to Reconnect Our lives, Our World.*

It is important for the leader to maintain an atmosphere of respectful silence of the group. Giving clear directions of the roles and time span deepens the experience of the participants. (60 minutes)

People sit in two concentric circles that face each other. The numbers in each are equal. (If the total numbers are uneven, the guide joins the inner circle, returning to his place in it after completing each stage of instructions.) Thus a double circle is formed of pairs sitting knee to knee, close enough to attend to each other without distraction, and on the same level. (If a mixture of chairs and floor cushions are used, the seat on the inner circle should be at the same height as the facing one in the outer circle.) Considerable concentration is required, so it is appropriate to treat the exercise as a kind of ritual and ask for silence as the double circle forms.

Those in the outer circle (facing in) speak for themselves at this point in time, out of their own experience; they stay seated in the same place. Those in the inner circle (facing out) are people of a future genera-tion (specify a date in fifty to two hundred years, not more). These future ones do not speak (until the end) and do move.

After each encounter, they rise, step back to move one place to the right, and sit again. In this way, the inner circle moves slowly clockwise while the outer circle is station-ary. Since the encounters it allows span many generations, we imagine that the double circle is occurring 'at a point outside of time.' Once the instructions are completed, the group enters this point outside of time by chanting a group sound- perhaps 'ah.'

Each of the four encounters is initiated by a query to the present-day person from the future being. It is imagined that this query is made telepathically, or heart to heart, although it is heard in the voice of the guide. The present-day people respond by speaking to the future ones directly in front of them, continuing for several minutes. The guide signals when it is time to con-clude, provides a brief silence (the pairs often bow to each other), then asks the future beings to move to the right. After the inner group is seated again, the new partners exchange silent greetings (again, usually a bow or 'namaste' with hands in gesture of prayer). Then the guide asks the next question (if necessary~ after reminding the future beings to remain silent).

The four questions, which the guide speaks on behalf of the future ones (and repeats for clarity), are given here.

1. Ancestor, I have been told about the difficult times in which you lived, the wars, the struggles, the humiliations, the fears, the longing for a homeland, and the shattered dreams....It is hard to believe. Was that really true? Tell me. What was it like for you in the midst of that? How did you feel?

2. Ancestor, we have songs and stories that still tell of what you and your friends did back then for peace. Now what I want to know is this: how did you start? You must have felt lonely and confused sometimes, especially at the beginning. Tell us about the part you played.

3. Ancestor, I know you didn't stop with those first actions on behalf of peace. Tell me, where did you find the strength and joy to continue working so hard, despite all the obstacles and discouragements?

When the third question has been answered, the future ones do not move on, but stay where they are. Now it is their turn to talk, while the other listens. They speak what is in their hearts after all they have just heard from their ancestors. What comes is often deep and surprising, so they take a good four to five minutes, and the pairs then exchange silent expressions of respect.

79

Now the body of the exercise, which took place 'at a point outside of time,' is over. To reenter ordinary time, where the future ones' roles are released, the group sounds again, as at the beginning; this provides a firm ritual closing. But the Double Circle does not disband yet. The last pairs stay together for another four or five minutes to reflect informally on the experience as a whole, the roles they played, the new perspectives that arose. This final conversation ends the exercise, but if time permits, it is rewarding to invite the whole group to share observations and insights.

From Leah's notes:

Our last activity together was an exercise that Carol adapted from Joanna Macy's book, *Coming Back to Life*. Our question of the elders was 'Tell me about what it was like in the year 2000 when the conflict was raging.'

Here's part of what Ester told me:

> *2000 was the time of our great suffering. Hatred had harmed us Jews and then I saw that it happened to the Palestinian people too. Let me tell you a story that happened to me a long time ago. A young Palestinian woman came to me with much hatred in her heart, and the hatred was transformed into love because we simply listened to her and loved her. Before I became a refugee, when I still lived as a girl with my parents in Germany, hatred wasn't allowed in my family. Even spinach I wasn't allowed to hate. Hatred is like a flame that we can fan or we can take away the oxygen... I never hated. If you allow hatred in it ruins you.*

At first I didn't realize that Ester was talking about what happened with Mary earlier that day, but suddenly I understood what was happening and Ester and I began to cry together in the power of that moment. I understood that Ester was telling me that we were part of the solution, our band of Compassionate Listeners at Hope Flowers School in the West Bank. In that moment I felt the power that each of us has on a daily basis to affect the lives of future generations when we choose to act from love.

Forgiveness Practice

Think of a relationship you have where there is need for forgiveness.

Choose to change the relationship and to stop the drain of your energy and attention.

State expectations you had which were not honored.

State what you would have preferred.

Acknowledge that the other did not meet those expectations and preferences.

Reaffirm your willingness to change the relationship . . . choose to cancel and let love go out to them as a human being with total responsibility for their own acts.

A Forgiveness Meditation
(This is an abbreviation of a Metta meditation weekend conducted by Sylvia Boornstein)

Metta Meditation begins with forgiving the easiest resentments and progresses to the most difficult. Ultimately, one learns to forgive one's self and all beings.

Reflect on what the word "forgiveness" means to you. What might it be to bring forgiveness into your life?

Begin by slowly bringing into your mind, into your heart, the image of someone close to you — someone you have no difficulty loving. Allow a picture, a feeling, a sense of that person.

Open to a sense of their presence and say, "I forgive you for whatever pain you may have caused me in the past, intentionally or unintentionally, through your words, your thoughts, your actions. However you may have caused me pain in the past, I forgive you."

Now bring forward in your mind a person toward whom you have had deep resentment. Can you soften toward them? Allow their presence to be felt. When you are ready, say to them: "I forgive you for whatever pain you may have caused me in the past, intentionally or unintentionally, through your words, your thoughts, your actions. However you may have caused me pain in the past, I forgive you."

Now gently bring into your mind, into your heart, the image, the sense, of someone who has resentment for you. Someone whose heart is closed to you — from whom you seek forgiveness.

"I ask your forgiveness. I ask to be let back into your heart. I ask that you forgive me for whatever pain I may have caused you in the past, intentionally or unintentionally, through my words, my thoughts, my actions. However I may have caused you pain in the past, I ask you to forgive me."

Allow youself to be forgiven. Soften your heart. Let it be.

And now gently turn to yourself in your own heart and say, "I forgive you," to you. Say, "I forgive you," to yourself.

Begin to share this miracle of forgiveness, of mercy and awareness. Let it extend out to all the people around you.

May all Beings, at all levels, on every plane, be free of pain and suffering. May we all be at peace.

13. CLOSING

At the close of each workshop we stand in a circle to offer thanks and dedicate the results of our work to benefit the earth and all beings. We acknowledge the gifts each individual has brought and is taking with her/him. It is a time to ground the experience and to set sights on our lives beyond the group: how we will enter our lives and what we intend to bring with us from this experience. It is a time of closing and a time of beginning.

GLOSSARY OF TERMS

COMPASSION

Compassion implies a non sentimental state of openheartedness without reservation. The Latin root of passion means "with pity." However, the present connotation of pity suggests a weakness on the part of the object. Compassion is an expanded state of awareness in which one does not focus on strong/weak, joy/pain; but is present without judgement.

DIALOGUE

The roots of the word come from the Greek words dia, meaning "through" and logos meaning "word," or "meaning." As William Isaacs describes it in his book, *Dialogue and the Art of Thinking Together*, dialogue is more than a conversation. It implies a flow of meaning. ".....dialogue is a conversation in which people think together in relationship. Thinking together implies that you no longer take your own position as final. You relax your grip on certainty and listen to the possibilities that result simply from being in a relationship with others — possibilities that might not have otherwise have occurred." (1999 p. 19)

In the formal dialogue group of which I have been a part, the purpose is to elevate relationship to a level of creativity and generation of new ideas which could not have been engendered except in that conversation. People speak to the center, and do not comment on what others have said except when it motivates something new. The circle provides a secure space of trust in which one can test assumptions and move beyond old patterns of thought to levels of new creativity.

The Israeli/Palestinian Livingroom Dialogue Group says "Good dialogue is an exchange of ideas and experiences that is so active, effective, and highly charged that it leaves none of the participants unchanged. It means learning to suspend one's opinions and judgements in order to truly listen to one another. It requires staying in the dialogue, even when one's closely held beliefs are challenged. It requires all participants to contribute from where they are — even half-formed ideas. It can result in divergent views converging, discovering a new social intelligence."

Lee Ross, a social psychology professor at Stanford who is part of the Stanford Center on Conflict and Negotiation says it is essential in a dialogue for each party to be able to say to the other what they perceive the other's interest to be. If they each can do this in a way that is satisfying to the other, then movement toward resolution can occur.

HOLARCHY

Author Arthur Koestler coined the word holon to refer to that which, being a whole in one context, is simultaneously a part in another. He saw that everything is at once a whole and a part of greater and greater wholes. Noting that hierarchies are composed of holons in increasing order of wholeness, Koestler pointed out that a more correct word for "hierarchy" is "holarchy." "Holarchy is simply an order of increasing holons representing an increase in wholeness and integrative capacity." This explanation was taken from the course materials, *Living on the Edge of Evolution*, developed by The Foundation for Global Community, Palo Alto, CA.

The symbol of the holarchy is used throughout this guidebook to imply compassion is the basic principle upon which all increasingly complex relationships and communication is based.

PRESENCE

Presence is a balanced state of awareness where attention is focussed on the present moment. It is often referred to as "Center." However, I see centering practices used as a way of bringing one to a state of Presence. It is a dynamic sate in which awareness is expanded to include one's inner state and outer fields of awareness. When listening compassionately, coming to a state of Presence allows one to have focussed awareness on all that is in the present moment — within and without.

PROJECTION

Projection is a process which occurs when we attribute characteristics to another which are parts of ourselves of which we are unaware. In relationships, we tend to be attracted to the qualities in people which are also in ourselves, but often underdeveloped. Opposites tend to be attracted to each other. Projection creates problems when we see others as having the characteristics we cannot accept in ourselves. Thich Nhat Hanh's poem, "Call Me By My True Names" is a startling exposure of the elements inherent in all humans. When they are unclaimed, we project them on to others, often making them our enemy.

QUALITIES

A quality is the superior characteristic or property of something. As used in this book, a life quality represents a deep attribute that characterizes an important part of your life. It is a distinguishing property of life, corresponding to something intangible that is of great value to you. The qualities you identify with define your wholeness.

These examples are adapted from an uncopyright list of qualities developed by the Psychosynthesis Institute of San Francisco in the 1970's.

Appreciation - Admiration - Beauty - Brotherhood - Bliss - Balance - Compassion - Communion - Calm - Courage - Communication - Connection - Creativity - Detachment - Energy - Enthusiasm - Eternity - Excellence - Entrepreneurship - Freedom - Faith - Friendship - Generosity - Goodwill - Goodness - Gratitude - Harmony - Humor - Humanitarianism - Infinity - Inclusiveness - Joy - Love - Light - Liberation - Order - Patience - Positiveness - Power - Quiet - Reality - Renewal - Resonance - Service - Serenity - Silence - Simplicity - Synthesis - Trust - Tranquility - Truth - Understanding - Vitality - Will - Wisdom - Wholeness - Wonder

REFLECTIVE LISTENING

Reflective listening is the restatement of a message. Mirroring means repeating verbatim what you have heard for the purpose of clarification. Reflective listening means indicating that one has received a message at all levels by extrapolating the essence of what you heard for the purpose of clarification and validation. It can be used with nonverbal messages. Often people take it to deeper levels by including the feelings they think were implied by the message. It is an invitation to the speaker to validate or clarify the intended meaning.

SHADOW

Biases which are hidden from consciousness become shadow. They can take the form of thoughts and behaviors of which we are unaware. We don't take full responsibility for our actions and tend to blame others when we act without awareness. The danger is that we are very likely to project these unconscious parts on to others through blame and condemnation.

REFERENCES

BIBLIOGRAPHY

Avruch, Kevin, Black, Peter W., Scimecca, Joseph A., ed., *Conflict Resolution: Cross-Cultural Perspectives*, Westport, CT: Praeger, 1991.

Avruch, Kevin, *Culture & Conflict Resolution*, Washington, DC: US Institute of Peace Press, 1998.

Bohm, David, *Wholeness and the Implicate Order*, London: Routledge, 1980.

Barach Bush, Robern A., Folger, Joseph P., *The Promise of Mediation: Responding to Conflict Through Empowerment and Recognition*, San Francisco: Jossey-Bass Publishers, 1994.

Braden, Gregg, *Walking Between the Worlds: The Science of Compassion*, Bellevue, WA: Radio Bookstore Press, 1997.

Csikszentmihalyi, Mihaly, *The Evolving Self: A Psychology for the Third Millennium*, NY: Harper Collins, 1993.

Childre, Doc & Paddison, Sara, *HeartMath® Discovery Program, Level One*, Boulder Creek, CA: Planetary Publishers of the HeartMath® System.

deBeauport, Elaine, with Diaz, Aura Sophia, *The Three Faces of Mind: Developing Your Mental, Emotional and Behavioral Intelligences*, Wheaton IL: Quest Books, 1996.

Diamond, Louise, *The Courage for Peace: Creating Harmony in Ourselves and the World*, Berkeley, CA: Conari Press, 2000.

Diamond, Louise, & McDonald, Ambassador John, *Multi-Track Diplomacy, A Systems Approach to Peace*, West Hartford, CT: Kumarian Press Inc., 1996.

Easwaran, Eknath, *The Compassionate Universe, The Power of the Individual to Heal the Environment*, Nilgri Press, Petaluma, CA: 1989.

Easwaran, Eknath, *Gandhi The Man: The Story of His Transformation*, Tomales, CA: Nilgri Press, 1997.

Flick, Deborah, Ph.D., *From Debate to Dialogue: Using the Understanding Process to Transform our Conversations*, Boulder, CO: Orchid Publications, 1998. dflick@quest.net

Gandhi, Mohandas K., *An Autobiography: The Story of My Experiments With Truth*, Boston: Beacon Press, 1957.

Glassman, Bernard, *Bearing Witness: A Zen Master's Lessons in Making Peace*, New York: Bell Tower, 1998.

Golman, Daniel, *Emotional Intelligence*, Bantam Books, New York, 1995.

Henderson, Michael, *Forgiveness: Breaking the Chain of Hate*, Wilsonville, OR: BookPartners, Inc. 1999.

Hock, Dee, *Birth of the Chaordic Age*, San Francisco: Berrett-Koehler Publishers, Inc., 1999.

Hoffman, Gene Knudsen, Green, Leah & Monroe, Cynthia, *Compassionate Listening: An Exploratory Sourcebook About Conflict Transformation*. 2001. To download this and other essays by Gene Knudsen Hoffman free of charge: <www.coopcomm.org>

Hopkins, Jeffrey, *Cultivating Compassion: A Buddhist Perspective*, New York: Broadway Books, 2001.

Houston, Jean, with Rubin, Margaret, *Manual for the Peacemakers: An Iroquois Legend to Heal Self and Society*, Quest Books, Wheaton, IL: 1995.

Huges, K.wind, Wolf, Linda, *Daughters of the Moon Sisters of the Sun: Young Women and Mentors on the Transition to Womanhood*, Stony Creek, CT: New Society Publishers, 1997

Isaacs, William, *Dialogue and the Art of Thinking Together,* NY: Random House, 1999.

Lederach, John Paul, *Building Peace: Sustainable Reconciliation in Divided Societies*, Tokyo, Japan: The United Nations University, 1995.

Macy, Joanna with Brown, Molly, *Coming Back to Life: Practices to Reconnect Our Lives, Our World*, Gabriola Island, BC, Canada: New Society Publishers, 1998.

Macy, Joanna, *Mutual Causality in Buddhism and General Systems Theory: The Dharma of Natural Systems,* Albany, NY: State University of New York Press, 1991.

Mennonite Conciliation Service, *Mediation and Reconciliation Facilitation Training Manual: Foundations and Skills for Constructive Conflict Transformation,* 21 South 12th Street, PO. Box 500, Akron, PA 17501-0500, (717) 859-3889, mcs@mccus.org

Mindell, Arnold, *Sitting in the Fire: Large Group Transformation Using Conflict and Diversity,* Portland, OR: Lao Tse Press, 1995.

Mindell, Arnold, T*he Leader as Martial Artist: Techniques and Strategies for Resolving Conflict and Creating Community*, San Francisco: Harper, 1992.

Mindell, Arnold, *Quantum Mind: The Edge Between Physics and Psychology*, Portland, OR: Lao Tse Press, 2000.

Nichol, Lee, ed., David Bohm *On Dialogue*, NY: Routledge, 1996.

Remen, Rachel Naomi, MD, *My Grandfather's Blessings: Stories of Strength, Refuge, and Belonging*, New York: Riverhead Books, a member of Penguin Putnam Inc., 2000.

Rosenberg, Marshall B., *NonViolent Communication: A Language of Compassion,* Del Mar, CA: Puddledancer Press, 1999.

Thich Nhat Hanh, *Call Me By My True Names*, Berkeley, CA: Parallax Press, 1999.

Thich Nhat Hanh, *Peace Is Every Step: The Path of Mindfulness in Everyday Life,* NY: Bantam Books, 1992.

Thich Nhat Hanh, *Being Peace*, Berkeley, CA: Parallax Press, 1987.

Tolle, Eckhart, *The Power of Now*, Novato, CA: New World Library, 1999.

Tutu, Desmond, *No Future Without Forgiveness*, NY: Doubleday, 1999.

Wiesenthal, Simon, *The Sunflower: On the Possibilities and Limits of Forgiveness*, NY: Shocken Books, 1997.

CONTACT INFORMATION

Cynthia Monroe, Director
Alaskans Listening to Alaskans About Subsistence
American Friends Service Committee
P. O. Box 110932
Anchorage, AK 99511
(907)278-2582
altas@alaska.net

The Center for Nonviolent Communication:
P.O. BOX 2662
Sherman TX 75091
(903) 893-3886
cnvc@compuserve.com
www.cnvc.org

Dialogue
www.uia.org/dialogue/webdial.htm

Selected Websites on Dialogue
uia.org/dialogue/webdial.htm

The Power of Dialogue
publicconversations.org

Fellowship of Reconciliation
Box 271
Nyak, NY 10960
(845) 358-4601
E-mail: FOR@forusa.org
www.forusa.org

Gene Knudsen Hoffman's Essays
Institute for Cooperative Communication Skills
Santa Barbara, CA
www.coopcomm.org

The Institute for Multi -Track Diplomacy (IMTD)
Dr. Louise Diamond, Executive Director
1819 H Street, NW, Suite1200
Washington, DC 20006
(206) 466-4605
E-mail: imtd@igc.apc.org

An inspirational 10-minute videocasette of Spring, 2002 MSNBC national news coverage of Jewish-Palestinian Dialogue in California will be mailed free of charge upon request. In VHS or PAL format, it illustrates the people, attitude, principles, atmosphere, sustained dedication, social outcomes, and hope. Contact:
Jewish/Palestinian Living Room Dialogue Group
1448 Cedarwood Dr.
San mateo, CA 94403
Voice (650) 574-8303 Fax (650) 573-1217
Web: http://traubman.igc.org
E-mail: LTRAUBMAN@igc.org

Learning Exercises
cgl.org/
OtherGrpResources.html#LearningExerGames

Joanna Macy
2812 Cherry St.
Berkeley, CA 94705
fax: (510) 649-9605

Makah Whaling Compassionate Listening
Jeff Smith
American Friends Service Committee
814 NE 40th St.
Seattle, WA 98105
Phone: (206)632-0500 FAX: 632-0500
e-mail: jsmith@afsc.org
www:july7coalition.org

Mid-East Citizen Diplomacy
P.O. Box 17
Indianola, WA 98342 USA
phone: (360) 297-2280
email: office@mideastdiplomacy.org
www.mideastdiplomacy.org

Rural Southern Voice for Peace
1898 Hannah Branch Rd.
Burnsville, North Carolina 28714
phone: (828) 675-5933
E-Mail: rsvp028714@yahoo.com

Date Due